Developing Africa?

Developing Africa?

New Horizons with Afrocentricity

Lehasa Moloi, Ph.D.

ANTHEM PRESS

Anthem Press
An imprint of Wimbledon Publishing Company
www.anthempress.com

This edition first published in UK and USA 2024
by ANTHEM PRESS
75–76 Blackfriars Road, London SE1 8HA, UK
or PO Box 9779, London SW19 7ZG, UK
and
244 Madison Ave #116, New York, NY 10016, USA

British Library Cataloguing-in-Publication Data
A catalogue record for this book is available from the British Library.

Library of Congress Cataloging-in-Publication Data
A catalog record for this book has been requested.
2023949401

ISBN-13: 978-1-83999-082-3 (Hbk)
ISBN-10: 1-83999-082-1 (Hbk)

Cover Credit: Art by Rre Lehlohonolo Shuping

This title is also available as an e-book.

CONTENTS

Foreword vii

Preface ix

Acknowledgements xi

Relevance of the Dialogue xiii

Overview of the Book xvii

1. Introduction 1

2. Theoretical Grounding: Afrocentricity's Approach to Development 15
   - Defining the Concept of Afrocentricity 17
   - Historical Roots of Afrocentricity 24
   - The Leitmotifs of Afrocentricity 29
     - Afrocentricity and its perspective on African history and Africa's contributions to ancient civilization 29
     - Afrocentricity's perspective on racism, slavery and colonialism 32
   - Afrocentricity and Its Critics 35
   - Afrocentricity's Response to Its Critics 38

3. Critique of Eurocentrism and a Mapping of African Development Initiatives 43
   - Eurocentrism in Development Studies: From Modernization to Neoliberalism 43
   - The Post–World War II Development Project and Its Implications for Africa 48
   - Africa's Journey with Development under Post-colonial Administrations 53
   - Mapping the Future of an African Development Trajectory beyond Eurocentrism 59

4. Afrocentricity on the Significance of African History for Development 65
Eurocentric Historiography and the Negation of Africa's Contribution to World Civilization 66
Afrocentric Historiography and the Restoration of Africa's Contribution to World Civilization 72
The African Renaissance and the African Development Challenge in Post-colonial Africa 81

5. Afrocentricity on the Significance of Culture in the Conceptualization of an African Development Paradigm 87
Defining the Concept of Culture 89
Eurocentrism, Culture and Development in Africa 92
Afrocentricity, Culture and Development in Africa 98

6. Afrocentricity on the Significance of African Agency in Development in Africa 105
Defining the Concept of African Agency 107
Problematic Agency and African Development Impasse 111
Afrocentricity, Agency and Development in Africa 113
Pan-Africanism 115
African nationalism 118
Concluding Remarks 121

Bibliography 123

Index 133

FOREWORD

Lehasa Moloi is one of those organic intellectuals whose ambition from his youth has been to tackle the issues related to what appears to be lagging material, political and social development of the African continent. Committed to the education of the masses that would include for him an investment in consciousness-raising among young college students, Moloi confronts the challenges of miseducation of the African with a revolutionary pedagogy based on African agency. He rescues us from the dead end of a misguided approach to development. While working on his doctorate with Sabelo Ndlovu-Gatsheni, perhaps the key African decolonial scholar, Moloi began to ask questions that prompted him to consider the historical agency of African people. It was not enough that one identifies and explains the decoloniality of power regarding the vestiges left by colonial oppressions, one had to sift through history to rediscover how Africans had conceived a world of relationships that were authentic and elastic enough to provide stability for thousands of years before the invasions of Europeans and Arabs.

Always ready to honour the academic guidance of Sabelo Ndlovu-Gatsheni, now the Chair of Epistemologies of the Global South at the University of Bayreuth, Moloi sought to take the route of African centeredness where the fundamental puzzle had to be found in how African people approached their own lived experiences in the context of contemporary challenges. In effect, the issues of epistemic freedom, decolonization and decoloniality in regard to 'development' had to be questioned from an Afrocentric perspective. What is it to be developed in African eyes? How must one see the constraints, restraints and complaints of Western authorities, whether from the Americas or Europe, about development in Africa?

Moloi has extended the discourse on 'development' in an urgent manner by refocusing theory and practice on African culture itself. To fulfil all societal ambitions of ethics, aesthetics, economics, technology and construction, there must be a collective sense of African agency where citizens are engaged in individual and group responses to external situations based on culture. Thus, Lehasa Moloi takes us beyond the destruction of the false facades of

Western thinking or Eastern thinking erected to conceal African capabilities. Africans do not have to follow Europe or Asia; it is possible to leap over the hurdles placed on our tracks and find our path tucked away in some corner of the African imagination.

It should be clear that Moloi is not rejecting the learning that can be gathered from all human contributions to knowledge; he recognizes that Africans can learn from others as others, like Picasso and Modigliani, borrowed artistic ideas from African arts. However, this new and sharper edge to development penetrates African history, testimonies, rituals and technologies to launch a world of African visionaries necessary for the future. They will be imbued with the Pan-African search for organic and authentic responses to development; thanks to Lehasa Moloi who has challenged us with an exit from the quagmire by asserting a radical Afrocentric thought that focuses on the African continent rather than the nebulous Global South.

Molefi Kete Asante is Professor at Temple University and the author of *The History of Africa*.

Molefi Kete Asante
Boston, 13 January 2023

PREFACE

This book is written for those who are interested in theoretical debates as they relate to the field of Development Studies. It is aimed at academics and all those who work in the field of development, politicians, policymakers and civil servants who need to familiarize themselves with key historical development debates, especially those relevant to Africa. The book takes an Afrocentric intellectual standpoint, grounded in the theory of Afrocentricity, in its interrogation of the ideas and processes of development in Africa. It also adopts a historical approach in its interrogation of the idea of African development as a by-product of political deliberations. This book is about how the discourse of development as a field of study needs to be reoriented to African-based epistemologies to dismantle coloniality, in opposition to the historical embeddedness of development discourse in Eurocentrism.

This book contests the limitation of the modern African understanding of Africa's journey with development to the period of the aftermath of World War II, to be specific, to President Harry S. Truman's 1949 Point Four programme.[1] Instead, that journey should be understood holistically. By this, I mean that Africa's engagement with development did not begin with the politics of the Euro-North American political bloc – the story of African development must take into consideration Africa's classical civilization, namely the Nile Valley civilization and its contributions to human civilization. Such an approach provides a more holistic interrogation and casts light on how Africa's history of greatness continues to be an inspiration even in modern times. Such an approach rejects the many reductionist lies and half-truths that undergird the modernist paradigm which seeks to portray African people as dependent beneficiaries of the colonial Euro-modernity framework. This framework has undermined the humanity of non-western people in general, and Africans in particular. The book pursues the tradition of decolonial epistemic reflections to oppose discourses that are riddled with a racist agenda towards those in the Global South, especially Africans.

1 Truman, Harry S. *Point Four.* Inaugural Address, 1949.

In the spirit of the pursuit of cognitive justice in the twenty-first century, this book argues that the discourse of development must be decolonized from hegemonic Eurocentric propaganda and needs to be framed from the viewpoint of those who have been seen as being on the receiving end, those projected as 'backwards' from a Eurocentric perspective.

I argue that African development discourses must be decolonized from parochial Western-centric lenses and must be reinterpreted within an Afrocentric history and culture. Africans need to assert the primacy of their agency as an expression of the African renaissance spirit. As Archibald Mafeje put it, Africans must think and do things for themselves to overcome domination by others.[2] In the same way, Molefi Kete Asante, the father of Afrocentricity, emphasizes that, 'since Africans have been moved off terms culturally, psychologically, economically, and historically, it is important that any assessment of the African condition in whatever situation or condition or estate be made from an Afrocentric location'.[3]

2 Archibald Mafeje, "Africanity: A Combative Ontology." *CODESRIA Bulletin* 1 & 4 (2000): 66–71.

3 Molefi Kete Asante, *An Afrocentric Manifesto: Toward an African Renaissance* (Cambridge and Oxford: Polity Press, 2007), 31.

ACKNOWLEDGEMENTS

There are many people I would like to thank for reading and offering reviews to this work. In particular, I thank the father of Afrocentricity, my mentor and inspiration, Professor Molefi Kete Asante. You challenged and changed my life for good. My encounter with the body of your work on Afrocentricity inaugurated my rebirth into Afrocentric scholarship. The opportunity to meet you and share a meal with you, and your humility, have taught me so much about life. I am forever indebted to you for showing me that to understand Africa one must be willing to look back to before the modern European invasion of Africa, which is not the beginning of African history, and must be willing to engage with the rise of Kemetic civilization as the first civilization in human history. Such an approach can ground students of African history in a more holistic manner than the many half-truths and lies about Africa taught by Europeans.

I also want to thank Professor Sabelo Ndlovu-Gatsheni, who laid a foundation for my epistemic liberation from Eurocentrism and encouraged me to speak with my own voice, and not fear. Mdala, I will never forget our first encounter in the seminar room in the Department of Development Studies at UNISA. Our conversation was the moment of my epistemic conversion from racist dominant epistemologies, as expressed through the Eurocentric canon of thought.

I want to express my wholehearted gratitude to the following:

- To my family, my late mother Mme Maseqethu Roselina Moloi, to my father Ntate Tubatsi Stephen Moloi, to my sisters and brothers and extended family, and in particular to my children, Pabala, Tlholo and Lekholokoe – let this be the inspiration.

RELEVANCE OF THE DIALOGUE

Notes on Afrocentricity, Decoloniality and the Reimagination of the World Free from Domination

Throughout this work, I have had the privilege of scholarly inputs from Professor Molefi Kete Asante, Chair of Africology at Temple University, widely acknowledged as the father of Afrocentricity. I also had the privilege of being reviewed by Professor Sabelo Ndlovu-Gatsheni, Chair of Epistemologies of the Global South at Bayreuth University, Germany, one of the leading scholars in decoloniality. Both have played an important role in shaping my theoretical outlook in this project, in which I engage with the complementarity between Afrocentricity and decoloniality as epistemic approaches to dismantling Eurocentrism, as the reason of terror, with its claims to being the universal voice and disregard of the particularity of context in knowledge production. By contrast, Afrocentricity as a liberatory paradigm seeks to advance the centrality of Africans in the interpretation of their own lives and argues that Africans must speak from their own cultural centre as an intellectual standpoint to dismantle the Eurocentric epistemic hegemony.

According to Asante, Afrocentricity is a paradigmatic intellectual perspective that privileges African agency within the context of African history and culture transcontinentally and trans-generationally.[4] Afrocentricity as a theory of social change primarily addresses a detailed investigation and questioning of the Eurocentric nature of knowledge. It wishes to avoid the personal and collective destruction of people of African descent and to reclaim an African cultural system as the coherent meeting point of every African cultural and historical past.[5]

For Ama Mazama, Afrocentricity is not merely a world view, or even a theory as such, but rather a paradigm that results in a reconceptualization of

4 Asante, *An Afrocentric Manifesto: Toward an African Renaissance.*

5 Ana Monteiro-Ferreira, *The Demise of the Inhumane: Afrocentricity, Modernism, and Postmodernism* (Albany, NY: Sunny Press, 2014).

the social and historical reality of Africans.[6] This idea is revolutionary because it casts ideas, concepts, events, personalities, and political and economic processes in the context of black people as subjects, and not as objects, basing all knowledge on the genuine interrogation of location. For this reason, Afrocentricity creates what ancient Egyptians referred to as a *djed*, and ancient Greeks called *stasis*, meaning, in both cases, a strong place to stand. Without such a strong place to stand on, African people easily become swallowed up in others' canons of thought; their culture and history are reduced to nothing.

The central thesis of this book is the idea that for African people to be remembered, for them to move forward from the many dehumanizing experiences of the past, the idea and practice of development in Africa needs to be grounded on a proper interpretation of history, and culture – it must activate African agency. Asante emphasizes that Africans must pursue in the most determined manner the practice of renaissance, that is, a rebirth of the culture, philosophy, traditions and values of the continent, not in some antiquated form, but in the spirit of creative responses to contemporary times.[7] Thus, the interrogation and reclaiming of the Nile Valley Civilization is a step in the right direction as part of an African Renaissance. In this book, I advance the claim that the quest for African development should not be grounded within the parochial lenses of the Euro-Modernity project. Rather, it must be understood within the context of the broader historical trajectory of the continent, beginning with the Nile Valley black civilization. Such an approach will lift the veil on how Euro-Modernity continues to represent a false foundation for the African development journey, which has suffered regression due to political interference.

Decoloniality as an epistemological and political movement in the twenty-first century seeks to deepen and widen decolonization movements in those spaces that experienced the effects of the slave trade, imperialism, colonialism, apartheid, neocolonialism and underdevelopment. This is because the domains of culture, the psyche, mind, language, aesthetics, religion and many others have remained colonized even after the official dismantlement of white colonial administration.[8] Moreover, decoloniality calls on intellectuals from imperialist countries to undertake a de-imperialization movement by re-examining their own imperialist histories and the harmful impact of those histories on the world.

---

6 Ama Mazama, *The Afrocentric Paradigm* (Trenton, NJ: Africa World Press, 2003).

7 Asante, *An Afrocentric Manifesto: Toward an African Renaissance.*

8 Sabelo J. Ndlovu-Gatsheni, "Decoloniality as the Future of Africa," *History Compass* 13, no. 10 (2015): 485–96.

Decoloniality was born out of the realization that the modern world is asymmetrical. The current world order is still sustained by colonial matrices of power. It also continues pedagogies and epistemologies of equilibrium that produce alienated Africans who are socialized into hating the very Africa that produced them, and into liking the Europe and America that rejects them. Decoloniality also seeks to address the key issues of consciousness. To advance its mission, decoloniality is framed around three key analytical units, namely coloniality of power, coloniality of knowledge and coloniality of being, as the markers to unmask the Eurocentric hegemonic cosmology. For this reason, for the purposes of this book, both Afrocentricity and decoloniality are read as complementary, especially when it comes to the critique of Euro-modernity as a hegemonic order.

It is important to note that decoloniality in terms of the scope of its focus is not exclusively African: its vision seeks to extend itself to the Global South as an ideological construct that includes Latin America, Asia and Africa. However, Afrocentricity by definition focuses primarily on the substance of African history, and culture, as well as an insistence on the centrality of African experiences as a base from which to decolonize and build an African awakening. This is pre-eminently in line with three facts. First, *Homo sapiens* emerged on the African continent. Second, human civilization emerged in Africa. Third, *Homo sapiens* spent three-fourths of the time that humans have been on earth as a species in Africa before they ever ventured out of Africa. For Afrocentrists, this means that interrogating African culture and history implies returning to interrogating human history itself. Therefore, European childishness is expressed in the way Europe centres the whole history of the world around Europe, when it is but the child of Africa. Thus, Europe is guilty of distorting the human record by employing an individualistic, selfish and imperialistic *Geist*.

The primary objective of this book, then, is to seek to reconceptualize the idea of African development from African values, grounded in an interrogation of African history and culture for an African renaissance. In this way, both Afrocentricity and decoloniality offer sharp reflective opportunities to reinterrogate the world as we have come to know it and to encourage us to shift the geopolitics of analysis as a way to think anew in our interrogation of life itself for human renewal.

OVERVIEW OF THE BOOK

This book is divided into six chapters.

Chapter 1

The chapter introduces the author and situates him in the context of his country of origin and the ideological struggles he encountered as both the student and the educator of Development Studies as an academic subject in his pursuit of cognitive justice, and search for relevance in the African context. The chapter introduces the key theoretical debates in the contestation of the ideas underpinning the discourse of development and lays the foundation for the ideological position taken by the author in the interrogation of Development Studies.

Chapter 2

This chapter introduces Afrocentricity as the overall guiding philosophical paradigm in the interrogation of the subject of Development Studies in Africa. The chapter defines the concept of Afrocentricity and traces its historical roots, leitmotifs, critics and response to the critics.

Chapter 3

This chapter delves deeper into the critique of Eurocentrism in the ideological make-up of the discourse of Development Studies in Africa, in particular, it exposes the flaws embedded in modernization theory, and by extension neoliberalism in the conceptualization of Africa's development ideal. The chapter also provides an overview of Africa's journey with development under the post-colonial epoch and also maps out the ideal future of African Development trajectory beyond Eurocentrism.

Chapter 4

This chapter discusses African history as an important cardinal in Afrocentricity in the remapping of African development trajectory. The chapter also provides a critique of Eurocentric historiography in its attempt to negate Africa's contribution to world civilization. Lastly, the chapter argues in favour of an Afrocentric narration of African history as a restorative mission to understand Africa's contribution to world civilization and the need to advance the African Renaissance in pursuit of the African development vision.

Chapter 5

This chapter discusses African culture as the second important cardinal in Afrocentricity in the re-conceptualization of the ideal African development vision. The chapter also provides a critique of how Eurocentric culture has distorted African ways of life and imposed monocultural ideas informed by western ideology in the advancement of the wrong kind of development.

Chapter 6

This is the last chapter of the book. It discusses the significance of asserting African agency as the third cardinal in Afrocentricity in pursuit of the dream of an Afrocentric development vision. The chapter discusses the concept of agency and its importance in the attainment and implementation of the African development vision.

Chapter 1

INTRODUCTION

As a young African writer from South Africa, I argue that the development project after World War II, rooted in the modernization paradigm, urgently needs to be reinterpreted in the context of, and against, the European Enlightenment project that traces its roots to the voyages of discovery from the late fourteenth century onwards. It has become abundantly clear that development ideas and practices grounded in this model will not bring about the development that Africa wants, but will continue to undermine African development initiatives and cement the Global North's domination agenda. I argue that African reconceptualization of its ideal development model should be grounded within the riches of African history and culture and needs to position Africans as their own agents, and not as objects. Only such a reconceptualization can liberate African development from parochial Eurocentric models.

We must shift the geography of reasoning and analysis away from a Eurocentric epistemology, towards African-centred epistemologies, in particular, using Afrocentricity as a revolutionary intellectual paradigm in our quest to liberate the discourse of development from the continuing bias towards the Eurocentric ideological framework. By doing so, we can work on a model that privileges African knowledge, informed by African history, culture and African agency, towards an African reawakening. I, therefore, deploy Afrocentricity as a relevant theoretical framework to relocate the interpretation of development to an African context to enable relevance to Africa. As Asante explains, Afrocentricity establishes an intellectual standpoint in which phenomena are viewed from the perspective of African people as centred within their own historical and cultural experiences.[1] Such a perspective enables African people to take control of their own lives and be their own agents. This will allow them to become subjects rather than objects of others' (under)development agenda. Afrocentricity as a paradigm enables

1 Molefi Kete Asante, "The Afrocentric Idea in Education," *Journal of Negro Education* 60 (1991): 170–9.

a re-examination of all dimensions of the dislocation of African people resulting from the imposition of Western thought, be it regarding culture, economics, psychology, health or religious ideas around African societies, and development in general. This interrogation and reflection will enable Africans to assert themselves epistemically, thus dismantling their entrapment in the Western epistemic colonization of the terms of reference, and enabling African people to speak as their own agents of the change that they desire, rather than merely existing as ideological dependants of the European canon of thought.[2]

The deployment of Afrocentricity in this book as a guiding framework enables the decolonization of Development Studies as an idea and practice in Africa from the Western epistemological hegemony. It sets a path for a re-articulation of the idea of development within an African setting. Afrocentricity therefore provides a relevant theoretical framework to enable African scholars to confront epistemic racism in the narrative of human development and to empower marginalized Africans to speak and define development from their own context.

After the successful completion of my master's degree in Development Studies in 2014, I felt the desire to pursue a PhD in Development Studies. Having had the privilege of being a student and later a lecturer in Development Studies, I began to reflect on my sense that there was something unsettling about the locus of enunciation and the historical framework which informs the theory of Development as a field of study. When I questioned the epistemological foundations which inform the discourse of development in Africa, I soon realized that Development Studies as an idea, process and practice was, and continues to be, grounded within the historical and social experiences of European countries, which imposed themselves as the standard of modern development practice. This is an aspect that I discuss at length in Chapter 3.

Historically, there have been two predominant perspectives which have shaped my reflections on the development discourse, namely mainstream Western development thought and counter-development discourses, including post-development thinking, African-centred ideals and decoloniality. The intellectual battle between mainstream discourses and counter-discourses regarding development as a field of study has affected how the process of development has been generally understood by scholars. Langdon sees 'Development Studies today as framed largely as a "Southern-focused" form of thinking, which they claim give the

2 Asante, "The Afrocentric Idea in Education," 172.

discipline a measure of inter-disciplinary legitimacy'.[3] Admittedly, there has been a consistent push to shift the geography of epistemology in Development Studies, but, demonstrably, the white gaze remains. Perhaps this is why Sumner[4] and Sylvester[5] posit that Development as a field of study fails to listen to the ideas of those in the Global South who are mostly affected by development agendas, Africans in particular. Therefore, in this book, I have chosen to deploy the theory of Afrocentricity to dismantle the hegemonic Eurocentric narrative of the idea and practice of development in Africa and to ensure that development becomes grounded in the experiences and knowledge of African people, rather than objectifying them.

The dilemma facing Development Studies today, as Ndlovu-Gatsheni[6] also contends, is the fact that this field of study remains ideologically embedded in Eurocentrism, and it has been shaped by the European colonial agenda, which has long masqueraded as a civilizing mission. This epistemic bias in the conceptualization of development has made it difficult for alternative visions of development to emerge, particularly in the Global South. Therefore, this book calls for the decolonization of the epistemology that informs the discourse of development. It emphasizes the need to reframe the conceptualization of development from an Afrocentric perspective to overcome the Eurocentric ideological bias which has perpetuated a culture of intellectual dependence amongst Africans and has limited their opportunities to see and understand the world differently. For this reason, Amin believes that 'Eurocentrism as a by-product of European conquest remains a modern ideological construct that consists of a bundle of Western prejudices about other people'.[7] Amin further posits that Eurocentrism gave birth to coloniality.[8] Latin American decolonial scholars such as Quijano,[9]

3 Jonathan Langdon, "Decolonizing Development Studies: Reflections on Critical Pedagogies in Action," *Canadian Journal of Development Studies* 34, no. 3 (2013): 385.

4 Andrew Sumner, "What Is Development Studies?" *Development in Practice* 16, no. 6 (2006): 644–50.

5 Christine Sylvester, "Development Studies and Postcolonial Studies: Disparate Tales of the 'Third World'," *Third World Quarterly* 20, no. 4 (1999): 703–21.

6 Sabelo J. Ndlovu-Gatsheni, *Coloniality of Power in Development Studies and the Impact of Global Imperial Designs*. Inaugural lecture (Pretoria: UNISA, AMRI: 2012), 48.

7 Samir Amin, *Eurocentrism: Modernity, Religion, and Democracy. A Critique of Eurocentrism and Culturalism* (New York, NY: Monthly Review Press, 2009), 177–8.

8 Amin, *Eurocentrism: Modernity, Religion, and Democracy.*

9 Anibal Quijano, "The Coloniality of Power and Social Classification," *Journal of World Systems* 6, no. 2 (2000): 342–86.

Grosfoguel,[10] Maldonado-Torres[11] and African decolonial scholar Ndlovu-Gatsheni[12] use the term 'coloniality' to highlight the dark side of modernity to reveal its negative impact outside of Europe and North America to unmask the mysterious perpetuation of the same system in the post-colonial political order.

Even though in the late 1950s Africa began a process of political decolonization which involved the overthrow of white colonial government administrations, beginning with Ghana in 1957, coloniality submerged the decolonization project into an emancipatory and reformist programme, rather than allowing it to become a revolutionary and anti-systemic project.

Kwame Nkrumah, the first president of Ghana, uses the concept 'neocolonialism' to describe a situation where former colonial empires continue to exercise control over their erstwhile colonies through indirect methods, such as the use of trade relations, as a mechanism to thwart growth.[13] Neocolonialism has come to be seen more generally as comprising well-coordinated strategies by former colonial European powers to impede genuinely independent progress in their former colonies. The main agenda is to ensure that the former colonies remain sources of low-priced raw materials and labour for their former imperial masters. Neocolonialism works as a crucial organizing process in international imperial schemes, sustaining the dominance of the Global North, and ensuring the perpetuity of the subalternity of the Global South.[14] Thus, development ideas and practices in Africa continue to be fashioned and controlled by global imperial designs.

Ndlovu-Gatsheni[15] has deployed the concept of 'colonial matrices of power', adopted from Anibal Quijano,[16] to highlight how these structuring processes impede development in Africa. There are four mechanisms through which the European powers have gained and still maintain control over the Global South.

10 Ramón Grosfoguel, "The Epistemic Decolonial Turn: Beyond Political-Economy Paradigms," *Cultural Studies* 21, nos. 2–3 (2007): 211–23; Ramón Grosfoguel, "Decolonizing Post-Colonial Studies and Paradigms of Political Economy: Transmodernity, Decolonial Thinking, and Global Coloniality," *Transmodernity: Journal of Peripheral Cultural Production of the Luso-Hispanic World* 1, no. 1 (2011): 1–34.

11 Nelson Maldonado-Torres, "On the Coloniality of Being." *Cultural Studies,* 21, nos. 2–3 (2007): 240–70.

12 Sabelo J. Ndlovu-Gatsheni, *Epistemic Freedom in Africa: Deprovincialization and Decolonization* (London: Routledge, 2018).

13 Kwame Nkrumah, *Neo-Colonialism: The Last Stage of Imperialism* (London: PANAF, 1965).

14 Walter D. Mignolo, "Introduction: Coloniality of Power and Decolonial Thinking," *Cultural Studies* 21, nos. 2–3 (2007): 155–67.

15 Ndlovu-Gatsheni, *Coloniality of Power.*

16 Quijano, "The Coloniality of Power."

The first mechanism is control of the *African economy*. This is made possible through the exploitation of African labour, land grabs and the control and pricing of Africa's natural resources. The Scramble for Africa, as mapped out during the Berlin Conference of 1884 to 1885, gave power to competing European nations to partition Africa as a physical environment, and to extract mineral resources for the sole benefit of colonial empires, without any regard for African people and their livelihood strategies.[17] The second mechanism is the control *of authority*. This includes the formation of military power to ensure the military superiority of the Global North and the legitimization of violence against indigenous African peoples.[18] The long history of colonial conquest has sharpened the skills of the former colonial powers in the art of violence. These countries have unmatched military equipment to enable them to sustain control through force. This has enabled the European powers to keep Africans and other countries under subjection to prevent them from attempting to topple colonial powers. The third mechanism is the *control of gender and sexuality*. This implies a reimagination of the definition of family in Eurocentric terms.[19,20] European colonization dismantled and undermined African traditional family structures and widely imposed a European civil marriage union system, which, among other things, forced Africans to register their marriages with the colonial government administration to be recognized.[21] The fourth mechanism is the *control of subjectivities and knowledge*. This includes the colonization of knowledge to ensure mind control over the subjects in the colonies to produce an inferiority complex, thus disrupting the indigenous culture.[22] For this reason, Africans continue to imbibe European colonial knowledge, perceiving it as superior, rather than drawing on their indigenous knowledge. This has perpetuated European epistemic domination over Africa, controlling Africans' imagination and interpretation of their reality.

I, therefore, employ the theory of Afrocentricity ideologically to reframe the negative impact of Eurocentrism and resultant coloniality, and how these shape African development discourses, with a view to decolonizing development discourse and giving Africans a voice to shape their own future.

---

17 Advice Viriri and Pascah Mungwini, "African Cosmology and the Duality of Western Hegemony: The Search for African Identity," *Journal of Pan African Studies* 3, no. 6 (March 2010): 28.

18 Ndlovu-Gatsheni, *Coloniality of Power*, 49.

19 Ndlovu-Gatsheni, *Coloniality of Power*, 49.

20 Quijano, "The Coloniality of Power."

21 Dare Arowolo, "The Effects of Western Civilization and Culture on Africa," *Afro-Asian Journal of Social Sciences* 1, no. 1, Fourth Quarter (2010): 1–14.

22 Grosfoguel, "The Epistemic Decolonial Turn," 214.

Afrocentricity as a revolutionary intellectual paradigm aims to advance the search for epistemic justice by ensuring that African people become grounded within the centrality of their own history and culture, and as agents of change in human history, with the aim of dismantling colonial oppression. Asante argues that since Africans have been dislodged from their own basis economically, politically, historically and psychologically, it is important to insist on their use of Afrocentric lenses to understand their lives.[23] Hence, the proposition of Afrocentricity is that Africans must look at knowledge from the perspective of Africa, Africans must be at the centre of their own historical and cultural experiences, and they must assert their own agency. Afrocentricity as a philosophical perspective emphasizes that African people must reground themselves within their own centre, which is, within their own history, culture, and must assert their own agency. In effect, there will be no decolonization unless Africans insist on their own agency – they will merely remain the puppets and spectators of others' shows.

In the opinion of Afrocentrists, Afrocentricity is not merely the antithesis of Eurocentrism. Instead, it argues for diversity in philosophical views, without building any hierarchy; in particular, it discourages the idea that a particular ideology must become the overarching view, the totalizing voice; rather, it encourages a diversity of perspectives, while emphasizing the centrality of African knowledge for African people. Afrocentricity challenges Eurocentrism and its narrative of human development, which elevates white supremacist ideas in its attempt to exclude Africans from the contributions they have made to human history and to present them as merely dependent beneficiaries of modernity, misconstrued as civilization from an Afrocentric perspective.

Thus, I seek to interrogate the interpellation of the idea, process and practice of development as expressed through Truman's interventionist development programme within European global imperial designs, which are disguised as an emancipatory and civilizational mission. My aim is to liberate development ideas and practices in Africa from a narrow European colonial epistemology and to reinterpret development from Afrocentric epistemological premises, as an expression of the pursuit of epistemic justice. The Euro-North American-centric agenda has continuously undermined African-based development initiatives, specifically the human-centred approach, in favour of a free-market economy that has led African states further into poverty in the aftermath of the nominal independence era that began in the late 1950s.

---

23 Asante, *An Afrocentric Manifesto: Toward an African Renaissance. Cambridge and Oxford: Polity Press*, 31.

The African development trajectory after independence was not conceptualized as part of an endogenous process rooted in African history, culture and identity, and asserting African agency. Instead, the idea, practice and discourse of development in Africa tends to regurgitate a Eurocentric modernist perspective aimed at colonizing Africans and turning them into European subjects. As Cheru points out, this interventionist view of development best expresses the 'imperial project' as it is framed in the Euro-North American propaganda of sustaining conquest over the Global South through a rhetoric of advancing humanitarianism.[24]

African development needs to be re-grounded in African people's own context to remain relevant, and it must provide solutions to the problems that people face, based on their own knowledge, experiences and culture in general. Therefore, African development needs to be contextualized within African people's history and their cultural perspectives to ensure relevance.

The provocative work that I am proposing undertakes to provide a critique of the mainstream development thinking and its deep interpellation within the Euro-North American modernist paradigm; to propose Afrocentricity as an African-centred perspective of development; to contribute to the body of knowledge on development debates by prioritizing African-centred knowledge within an African context and to confront the resilient 'white gaze' (epistemic racism) embedded in the field of Development Studies, with a view to contributing to epistemic justice for those who have been pushed to the periphery.

As a guide to this book, I have chosen the following questions as markers along the Afrocentric path towards the reimagination of an African development ideal:

- What is the origin and genealogy of development discourse and practice?
- How can Afrocentricity as a revolutionary paradigm be deployed to decolonize development discourse and practice in Africa?
- What contributions can be derived from shifting the geography of reason from Eurocentric to African-centred thinking in the field of Development Studies?
- How can the 'white gaze' embedded in the field of Development Studies be confronted to attain epistemic justice and freedom for Africans?

Afrocentricity as a theory is influenced among others by the Civil Rights Movement in the United States of America and the Black Consciousness

24 Fantu Cheru, "Development in Africa: The Imperial Project versus the National Project and the Need for Policy Space," *Review of African Political Economy* 120 (2009): 275–8.

Movement of South Africa. It was nurtured by Africology department at Temple University School in Philadelphia, Pennsylvania, where the philosophy was institutionalized by a group of African intellectuals frequently referred to as the Temple Circle of scholars. These scholars included C. Tsehloane Keto, Theophile Obenga, Ama Mazama, and Molefi Kete Asante, the pioneer theorist of the group.

In his core works, *Afrocentricity: The Theory of Social Change,*[25] *Kemet, Afrocentricity and Knowledge,*[26] *The Afrocentric Idea,*[27] *The Afrocentric Manifesto*[28] and *African Pyramids of Knowledge,*[29] Asante articulated and refined the ideas and principles underpinning this paradigm. It is important to note that Afrocentricity has been articulated and used at various levels: as a philosophical movement,[30] as an ideological standpoint[31] and as an epistemological and a methodological approach to African discourses.[32,33] The common thread connecting these levels is their call for cognitive justice and the change in how epistemology is produced, to oppose the unfair use of one epistemology to dominate over others, particularly the epistemology emerging from Eurocentrism.

The primary premise of Afrocentricity is the centrality of African experiences in all dimensions of life, in order to dismantle oppressive discourses. Afrocentricity emerged in part as an approach to combat the ontological, epistemological and methodological hegemony arising from Eurocentrism as an institutionalized paradigm (also referred to as Western centrism). At the centre of Afrocentricity is the rejection of the long-held notion that the European canon of thought must assume the status of a 'universal knowledge' that transcends time and space. Thus, Afrocentricity holds that every knowledge emerges within a particular context and that contexts are

25 Molefi Kete Asante, *Afrocentricity: The Theory of Social Change* (New York, NY: Amule, 1980).

26 Molefi Kete Asante, *Kemet, Afrocentricity and Knowledge* (Trenton, NJ: Africa World Press, 1990).

27 Molefi Kete Asante, *The Afrocentric Idea* (revised expanded ed.) (Philadelphia, PA: Temple University Press, 1998).

28 Asante, *An Afrocentric Manifesto.*

29 Molefi Kete Asante, *African Pyramids of Knowledge: Kemet, Afrocentricity and Africology* (New York, NY: Universal Write Publications LLC, 2015).

30 Tony Anderson, "Blowing Smoke: Exposing Empty Criticism of Afrocentricity," in *Molefi Kete Asante: In Praise and Criticism*, ed. Dhyana Ziegler (Nashville, TN: Winston, 1995), 115–24.

31 Maulana Karenga, *Introduction to Black Studies*, 3rd ed. (Los Angeles, CA: University of Sankore Press, 2002).

32 Asante, *Kemet, Afrocentricity and Knowledge.*

33 Mazama, Ama, "The Afrocentric Paradigm: Contours and Definitions," *Journal of Black Studies* 31, no. 4 (2001): 387–405.

multiplicitous. Hence, Afrocentricity rejects the idea that one particularity may pretend to represent all particulars. Such a view, according to Afrocentrists, would be a major distortion which would serve an agenda of the domination of others, just as Eurocentrism has done. For Afrocentrists, all centres of knowledge must be respected as valid for the people they serve. One cannot divest a people of its central position in its own narrative and make that people an appendage to others without a history. Africa was home to the earliest members of *Homo sapiens*, so why should African people not see themselves in the centre of their own narratives?

Afrocentricity suggests that African development should be informed by Africans as agents, rather than as dependent beneficiaries of European-conceptualized ideas of development. Therefore, Afrocentricity aims to ensure that the discourse and practice of development in Africa overcome what Chambers has termed the 'outsider's perspective'.[34] When development is defined by a Euro-North American agenda, it expresses hegemonic practices and renders Africans mere objects – passive recipients in the process.

Asante outlines five key principles or characteristics underlying the qualitative nature of Afrocentricity.[35] The first principle is that Afrocentricity argues that no phenomenon can be fully understood without locating it first. A phenomenon must be studied and analysed in relation to its psychological time and space. It must always be located. This implies that even the study of development and especially its practice in Africa must be contextualized in the African milieu. Any effort to interpret and understand development outside of the historical journey of the people involved creates a dislocating effect and undermines the beneficiaries of such a process. Therefore, all the data relating to the development discourse must be examined from the standpoint of Africans as subjects and human agents, and not as objects to be developed. The second principle of Afrocentricity is that it considers phenomena to be diverse and dynamic – in motion. Thus, it is necessary to note carefully and record accurately the location of phenomena, even in the midst of fluctuations. This means that a researcher must be clear ideologically about where he or she stands in this process of research. The concept of development should be regarded as fluid rather than fixed because it deals with people's existential realities in their own context. It is important for researchers to immerse themselves in the worldview and the experiences of those who are studied. The third principle is that Afrocentricity is a form of cultural criticism that investigates the etymological uses of words and terms in order

34 Robert Chambers, *Rural Development: Putting the Last First* (Harlow: Prentice Hall, 1983), 2–3.

35 Molefi Kete Asante, *Afrocentricity*, 2009 [Online] 2.

to investigate the source of an author's location. This allows researchers to identify the connection of ideas with actions, and actions with ideas to recognize clearly what is detrimental, and ineffective, versus what is imaginative and transformative at the political and economic levels of those being researched. This implies that the Eurocentric notion of development as an injection of European values and systems in a non-European context, as suggested by Lerner,[36] must be interrogated and resisted as a colonial practice which marginalizes other knowledge systems and worldviews, and must be challenged by relocating the analysis within Africa as a base. The fourth principle of Afrocentricity is that it seeks to unmask unfair power dynamics, in particular, as they relate to knowledge production, which privileges the colonial master's narratives over African voices and experiences. Thus, Afrocentricity is perspectivist because it attempts to provide the endogenous knowledge to dismantle imposed knowledge. For this reason, development as a process must end the dependency of those formerly colonized on the colonizers and enable those formerly colonized to define their own destiny. The fifth and final principle is that Afrocentricity locates the ingenious structures of a system of economics, bureau of politics, policy of government and expression of cultural form in the attitude, direction and language of the phenomena under review, whether these are texts, institutions, personalities, interaction or events. In this way, the theory enables the qualitative inquiry of the people who are researched to understand the dynamics at the centre of their lives. This implies that an inquiry into development discourse(s) should not be seen as an exogenous process but as an endogenous one.

The project of development (all too often underdevelopment) rooted in the modernization paradigm in the era after World War II (from 1945 onwards) has been criticized for its embeddedness in the Eurocentric modernist paradigm and negative consequences for the material conditions of its victims in the Global South, and in Africa in particular.[37–42]

---

36 Daniel Lerner, *The Passing of Traditional Society: Modernizing the Middle East* (Glencoe, IL: Free Press, 1958).

37 Langdon, "Decolonizing Development Studies."

38 Arturo Escobar, *Encountering Development: The Making and Unmaking of the Third World* (Princeton, NJ: Princeton University Press, 1995).

39 Ndlovu-Gatsheni, *Coloniality of Power.*

40 Sabelo J. Ndlovu-Gatsheni, "The African Idea of Development," in *Routledge Handbook of African Development*, eds. Tony Binns, Kenneth Lynch, and Etienne Nel (London: Routledge, 2017), 1–16.

41 Walter Rodney, *How Europe Underdeveloped Africa* (London: Bogle-L'Ouverture, 1972).

42 Wolfgang, E. Sachs, *The Development Dictionary: A Guide to Knowledge as Power* (Johannesburg: Witwatersrand University Press, 1992).

According to Langdon, the critique of development discourse and practice falls into two categories, which emerged over time.[43] The first category is premised on material criticism, which generally focuses on how what was long considered the philanthropic character of development has reinvigorated and sustained the colonial structure of centre/periphery relations. In other words, the idea of development which was rooted in the post–World War II modernist project was built on the wrong foundations, which cemented European domination and the exploitation of non-European nations. This is visible in the writings of the dependency school of thought which arose during the late 1950s as a result of discontent with the dismal failure of the modernization project.[44,45] Although the theorists in this school did not adhere to homogenous ideas in their opposition of modernization theory, they shared several common assumptions. Namkoong[46] and Hettne[47] summarize four views commonly held by dependency theorists. In the first place, dependency theorists often refute the claim of modernists that underdevelopment was created by internal factors in the underdeveloped countries themselves; instead, they argue that the causes of underdevelopment are external and emanate from the exploitative nature of the relationship of the 'underdeveloped' countries with developed countries. Second, they believe that the world is divided into two parts: the centre (which includes industrialized/affluent Western countries) and the periphery (which includes underdeveloped, unindustrialized and poor countries in the Global South). Third, unequal exchange in international trade between the centre and the periphery is the main reason for underdevelopment in the periphery. Fourth, as a strategy or a way forward, they recommend that the Global South in general, and Africa in particular, should delink from European development models and strive for self-reliance to re-emerge.

Although the development project in the 1980s led to the globalization project that prioritizes free markets, the privatization of properties and individual incentives, it was still rooted within the modernization project

43 Langdon, "Decolonizing Development Studies," 389.

44 Paul A. Baran, *The Political Economy of Growth* (New York, NY: Monthly Review Press, 1957).

45 Immanuel Wallerstein, *The Modern World System: Capitalist Agriculture and the Origin of the European World-Economy in the Sixteenth Century* (New York, NY: Academic Press, 1974).

46 Young Namkoong, "Dependency Theory: Concepts, Classification, and Criticism," *International Study Review* 2, no. 1 (1999): 125.

47 Bjorn Hettne, "The Development of Development Theory," *Acta Sociologica* 26, nos. 3/4 (1983): 253.

that fortified Western dominance.[48] The manifestation of centre/periphery exploitation continued in Africa during the 1980s through the conditions attached to the economic structural adjustment policies (ESAPs) that were recommended and implemented.[49,50] Despite the failure of these policies, the International Financial Institutions (IFIs) continued to impose them on Africa into the 1990s, leaving Africa deeply enmeshed in debt.[51]

The second category of criticisms levelled at development discourses addresses the link between knowledge hierarchies and power.[52] The very notion of development expresses a European worldview which fails to give non-Europeans an avenue to share their experiences and knowledge to enrich Development Studies. Brohman posits that grand theorization in Development Studies was a by-product of Western epistemology, and it suffers from a reductionist bias, as simplistic mono-causal explanations are provided to offer grand solutions to complex development challenges.[53] Lushaba,[54] Ndlovu-Gatsheni[55] and Rist[56] have all criticized Development Studies as a discipline that suffers from coloniality of power and the hegemony of a Eurocentric bias, which is expressed in the fact that ideas such as progress and development reflect only a European imagination.

Davis explains that the development field must be challenged to reject the preconceived colonial ideas and models; hence, development scholars must unlearn universalized ideas and treat development as a process which is contextual.[57] There is, therefore, an urgent need to reinvent Development Studies to accommodate the sociocultural, political, economic

---

48 Mogens Buch-Hansen and Laurids S. Lauridsen, "The Past, Present and Future of Development Studies," *Forum for Development Studies* 39, no. 3 (2012): 293–300.

49 Anthony Baah, *History of African Development Initiatives*, paper presented at the African Labour Research Network (Johannesburg, 2003).

50 Jephias Matunhu, "A Critique of Modernization and Dependency Theories in Africa: Critical Assessment," *African Journal of History and Culture* 3, no. 5 (2011): 65–67.

51 Baah, *History of African Development Initiatives*, 6.

52 Langdon, "Decolonizing Development Studies," 389.

53 John Brohman, "Universalism, Eurocentrism, and Ideological Bias in Development Studies: From Modernisation to Neoliberalism," *Third World Quarterly* 16, no. 1 (1995): 121–40.

54 Lwazi Siyabonga Lushaba, *Development as Modernity, Modernity as Development* (Dakar: CODESRIA, 2009).

55 Ndlovu-Gatsheni, "The African Idea of Development."

56 Gilbert Rist, *The History of Development: From Western Origin to Global Faith* (London: Zed Books, 2002).

57 Diane E. Davis, "Unlearning Languages of Development: From Rhetoric to Realism in Recent Studies of Latin America," *Latin American Research Review* 27 (1992): 151–68.

and environmental contexts of the various societies to subvert the fixity of Eurocentric idealism. Post-development scholars such as Escobar[58] and Sachs[59] have therefore called for the reframing of Development Studies within the sociopolitical cultural contexts of non-Western societies[60]; in this way, epistemic racism rooted in Eurocentric bias could be overcome.

Baah,[61] Chukwuokolo[62] and Matunhu[63] argue that if Africa is to progress, it must reframe its understanding of development within its own context and not just transplant European experiences and ideas. According to Asante, African minds must be relocated from Euro-dogmas and contextualized within the African cultural setting, from which problems can be properly defined as a way to find relevant solutions.[64]

The debates on decolonization in Africa have regained momentum in the twenty-first century, and African universities now face the mammoth challenge to decolonize their educational content and curricula to reflect the existential realities of the marginalized. At the centre of the decolonization debates lies the search for contextual relevance and the need to liberate academic discourses from the Eurocentric epistemic racism that has marginalized other ways of knowing.

Mafeje suggests that social science disciplines are entrapped in what he calls an 'epistemology of alterity',[65] which refers to a scholarship entrenched in the Western canon of thought.[66] To overcome this tendency, Mafeje argues that Africans must insist on thinking and doing things for themselves, while not rejecting a willingness to collaborate with others.[67]

I, therefore, propose that for development discourse to be truly beneficial for Africans, it needs to be sensitized to the African context, meaning that it must take into consideration the history and culture of African people, and must activate the agency of African people. The entry to development debates

---

58 Escobar, *Encountering Development.*

59 Sachs, *The Development Dictionary.*

60 Sachs, W. E. 1992. *The Development Dictionary.*

61 Baah, *History of African Development Initiatives.*

62 J. Chodizie Chukwuokolo, "Afrocentrism or Eurocentrism: The Dilemma of African Development," *OGIRISI: New Journal of African Studies* 6, no. 1 (2009): 24–39.

63 Matunhu, "A Critique of Modernization."

64 Asante, "The Afrocentric Idea in Education."

65 Mafeje, "Africanity: A Combative Ontology," cited in Nontyatyambo P. Dastile, "Beyond Euro-Western Dominance: An African-Centred Decolonial Paradigm," *Africanus Journal of Development Studies* 43, no. 2 (2013): 74.

66 Dastile, "Beyond Euro-Western Dominance," 97.

67 Mafeje, "Africanity."

should not legitimize Eurocentrism as a universal model, but should rather see it as only one particular geopolitical viewpoint in the context of history. It is in this context that the idea and practice of development in Africa should speak to African problems in the context of the continent's historical experiences of European hegemony. Development Studies should not merely be understood as a regurgitation of Western thought in Africa but need to be grounded in an African worldview. Here, I do not seek to reinvent the wheel – rather, I am joining the group of Afrocentric theorists who argue for an Afrocentric awakening and revivalism as a way to heal from the colonial dismemberment.

I argue that the European historical development politics have shaped the notions undergirding the discourse of development in Africa and have distorted Africa's desire to redevelop in the aftermath of the post-independence era to date. What should happen is that the alternative development strategies adopted by African leaders following the independence era should be analysed and discussed according to their Afrocentric orientation to rebuild the former greatness of Africa. In this way, I am lending my voice to the debates on the development of discourse and practice.

Chapter 2

THEORETICAL GROUNDING: AFROCENTRICITY'S APPROACH TO DEVELOPMENT

Afrocentricity has become the dominant intellectual paradigm in the analysis of African phenomena in the last two decades, if not longer. Afrocentricity was conceptualized and developed through the skilful writings of Molefi Kete Asante, who is the leading theorist, and Chair of the Africology and African American Studies Department at Temple University (Philadelphia, Pennsylvania), which is considered the construct's intellectual home. The primary role of Afrocentricity has been to depose the dominant Eurocentric paradigm, which has been identified as a leading cause of the de-centring and dislocation of Africans from their own historical and cultural experiences.

Thus, Afrocentricity proposes the relocation and the re-centring of African persons within their own historical, political and cultural context as a key for their liberation from Eurocentric epistemic domination. More than anything else, Afrocentricity is a paradigm of agency and action; it seeks to decentre Europe, its knowledge system and its hegemonic practices from the centre of African reality and replace it with an African-based knowledge system, informed by African history and culture, as framed within the lived experiences of African people transcontinentally and trans-generationally. This implies that establishing the intellectual location of the researcher is indispensable to any examination of African people's culture, politics, spirituality, economics and psychology in general. It is critical to understand in this study that Afrocentricity is not articulated as a fixed corpus of ideas or perspectives, or as a closed system of beliefs.[1]

Since the advent of the colonization of Africa by Europe, starting in the early fifteenth century, information regarding the continent of Africa and its people has been articulated from a European point of view, with the effect of submerging an African world view. The call for the liberation of

1 Asante, *An Afrocentric Manifesto: Toward an African Renaissance.*

Africans from the European political hegemony and subsequent neocolonial ties in the post-independence era has coincided with calls for a liberation of epistemology. The challenge that the newly independent nation-states faced was how to develop themselves by improving the quality of life for African people. Regarding education, the main challenge was to liberate African minds from the ravages of the legacy of the colonial knowledge system. Ndlovu-Gatsheni puts it as follows:

> [B]ecause of the longstanding consequences of modernity, enslavement and colonialism, African people have been reproduced as objects of development within the Eurocentric historiography. Colonialism disrupted their societal order and re-oriented them on the false trajectory, which objectified them as backward people, as a people who are only acted upon rather than acting, and as a people without culture and history.[2]

Ndlovu-Gatsheni[3] agrees with the view expressed by Asante,[4] stating that 'although colonization of Africans has ended (as a direct control of African political administration), Africans remain psychologically dominated'.[5] Having had their minds colonized by European invaders, Africans have remained colonial subjects relying on the colonial library to seek an understanding of themselves, which has further deepened their dislocation. The relocation of an African mindset into the African historical and cultural context is the solution to usher in the liberation of Africa's people in pursuit of African decolonization.

Against this background, therefore, Afrocentricity seeks to restore African ontological density by deposing the destructive effects of Eurocentric historiography. However, it is crucial to note that while the call to reassert an African perspective and agency was made earlier, it is Asante who systematically introduced Afrocentricity as a paradigm into academic discourse. Many Africans on the continent, as well as African American historians, writers, poets, musicians and political activists before Asante's time, have made the point that for Africans, particularly in America and in other diasporas, to be fully liberated, they must trace their genealogy within the context of Kemet (Egypt) and, in particular, the Nile Valley Civilization.

---

2 Ndlovu-Gatsheni, *Epistemic Freedom in Africa*, 1.
3 Ndlovu-Gatsheni, *Epistemic Freedom in Africa*, 10.
4 Asante, *An Afrocentric Manifesto: Toward an African Renaissance*, 10.
5 Ndlovu-Gatsheni, *Epistemic Freedom in Africa*, 3.

However, this call did not materialize as a philosophical concept and a paradigm in academia until the 1980s, when Asante published his book *Afrocentricity: The Theory of Social Change.*[6] The book ushered in a new era; it framed Afrocentricity as a paradigm and gave it status in academia as a legitimate paradigm for the study of African phenomena. Thus, Asante offers Afrocentricity as an ethical ideological standpoint that positions Africans as subjects in their own development, rather than as objects, and that inaugurates a relevant ideological basis for explanations of African historical experiences.[7]

Defining the Concept of Afrocentricity

Asante defines Afrocentricity as follows:

> Afrocentricity is a mode of thought and action in which the centrality of African interests, values, and perspectives predominate. Regarding theory, it is the placing of African people in the center of any analysis of African phenomena.[8]

The key aspect in Asante's definition is 'the assertion of African agency within the lived experiences of African people in the context of their culture and history, regardless of which phenomena are analysed'.[9] Afrocentricity is, therefore, a groundbreaking intellectual perspective, proposed as a constructural adjustment to African disorientation, de-centredness and the lack of agency resulting from the Eurocentric hegemony.[10]

Monteiro-Ferreira explains that

> Afrocentricity is primarily addressed to a detailed investigation and questioning of the Eurocentric nature of knowledge; to avoid personal and collective destruction of people of African descent; to reclaim an African cultural system as a coherent meeting point of every African cultural and historical past.[11]

6 Asante, *Afrocentricity: The Theory of Social Change.*
7 Asante, *The Afrocentric Idea* (revised expanded ed.), xiii.
8 Molefi Kete Asante, *Afrocentricity: The Theory of Social Change* (revised, expanded ed.) (Chicago, IL: African American Images, 2003), 2.
9 Asante, "The Afrocentric Idea in Education," 172.
10 Asante, *Afrocentricity* [Online].
11 Monteiro-Ferreira, *The Demise of the Inhumane*, 1–2.

This idea starts with the recognition that Eurocentrism as a particular perspective remains 'a normal expression of culture',[12] as far as Europeans are concerned, but is in fact 'abnormal if it imposes its cultural particularity as "universal" while denying and degrading other cultural views'.[13] In opposing the hegemonic intellectual climate that has been normalized by Eurocentrism, Afrocentricity aims to transmute human reality by steering in openness towards a cultural diversity that cannot exist without unlocking our minds to accepting an expansion of our consciousness.[14] As he seeks to outline his ideological position, Asante explains: 'I seek to overthrow parochialism, provincialism, and narrow Wotanic visions of the world by demonstrating the usefulness of an Afrocentric approach, based on beginning with ancient Kemet, to question knowledge.'[15]

Afrocentricity recognizes that the arrogance characterizing Eurocentric scholarship arises from its unwillingness to learn (and indeed its fear of learning) from others, as doing so might pose a threat to the European hegemony. Thus, Eurocentrism has plunged the Global North into an epistemic racist posture that has led to self-praise and the plague of egoism that has denied Africans the platform to speak. In this context, Asante argues that the primitive hold that Europe once held over the world is crashing into the barricades of history, and we are at a new turn in the world of ideas and knowledge.[16] The former enslaved are using every means possible to foster their revolt against oppression; and in revolt, they overturn both their own victimization and oppression and the idea that Europe is supreme.[17] For this reason, the emergence of Afrocentricity, as Asante contends, is a call to challenge the continuation of white racial dominion over all symbols and social systems, by opposing archaic structures of race based on the imposition of a particular cultural reality as if it were universal.[18]

In this book, Afrocentricity is presented as an alternative perspective that seeks to restore African people within their own historical and cultural landscape to overcome the cultural crisis created by Europe's epistemic arrogance. Asante emphasizes that 'it becomes essential to accept the subject

---

12 Asante, *Afrocentricity* [Online].

13 Asante, *Afrocentricity: The Theory of Social Change* (revised, expanded ed.), 61.

14 Asante, *African Pyramids of Knowledge*, vii.

15 Asante, *African Pyramids of Knowledge*, vii.

16 Asante, *African Pyramids of Knowledge*, ix.

17 Asante, *African Pyramids of Knowledge*, ix.

18 Molefi Kete Asante, "Afrocentricity and History: Mediating the Meaning of Culture in Western Society," *Souls: Critical Journal of Black Politics & Culture* 2, no. 3 (2000): 50.

position of Africans within the context of their historical realities if progress is to be made in interpretation, analysis, synthesis, or construction'.[19]

From an Afrocentric perspective, Eurocentrism has denied and alienated African culture, de-Africanized the consciousness of Africans and arrested their economic and cultural development; it, therefore, represents a potent threat to the cultural, social, economic and political development of Africans.[20] In his further criticism of Eurocentrism, Asante emphasizes that the main problem with the Eurocentric supremacist way of thinking has been its intolerance of other ways of knowing; thus, Eurocentrism has become self-absorbed and trapped in the notion that it represents the categorical 'universal' for the world.[21] He adds that 'everywhere Europe has sought domination, defeat, ethnic cleansing, and conquest and in no way has it sought co-existence with non-European peoples'.[22] It is because of this quest by the Global North for domination that African people, in the 500 years of their domination, have become removed from their own terms and speak using European terms as theirs. Hence, Afrocentricity seeks to communicate the need to relocate, reassert and re-ground African people historically, economically, socially, politically and philosophically as a way to overcome their dislocation. Mazama adds that African dislocation resulting from Eurocentric intellectual dominance has led Africans willingly to accept footnote status in the white man's book.[23]

Asante laments that

> [...] if there is anything Africans have lost under European domination, it is their cultural centeredness; that is, we have been moved from our own platforms. This means we cannot truly be ourselves or know our potential since we exist in a borrowed space and have become the spectators of a show that defines us without our own input.[24]

This implies that without an understanding of our historical past, we will remain trapped as objects of European experimentation. Asante comments:

> [...] to say we are de-centered means essentially that we have lost our own cultural footing and have become other than our cultural and

---

19 Asante, "Afrocentricity and History," 51.

20 Asante, *Kemet, Afrocentricity, and Knowledge.*

21 Asante, "Afrocentricity and History," 53.

22 Asante, "Afrocentricity and History," 53.

23 Mazama, "The Afrocentric Paradigm: Contours and Definitions," 387.

24 Asante, *The Afrocentric Idea* (revised, expanded ed.), 8.

> political origins dislocated and disoriented. We are therefore essentially insane, that is, living an absurdity from which we will never be able to free our minds until we return to the source.[25]

Mazama expresses a similar view,[26] acknowledging that Africans are dislocated – having lost sight of themselves in the midst of European decadence and madness, it has become increasingly difficult for them to orient their lives in a positive and constructive manner. Against this dislocation, Afrocentricity proposes that Africans must be restored to, and placed within, their own historical and cultural setting as a way to overcome their de-centredness and disorientation.

Therefore, the primary objective of Afrocentricity is to give Africans back their victorious consciousness. It also means locating 'the European voice and perspective as just one among many, and not necessarily as the wisest one'.[27] It is a perspective that makes a call on all Africans, regardless of where they are located in the world. It calls on them to be relocated ideologically within their historical and cultural setting. In academic circles, Afrocentricity can best be understood as a paradigm that seeks to enthrone the centrality of African experiences as a base from which African people's reality should be interpreted.

Asante (2017:24) argues that

> [...] until we as Africans reset the social sciences, humanities, natural sciences and arts more closely to our own historical narratives we will continue to assume the role of junior brother and sister to other world narratives as if our own experiences, that is, those of our ancestors are less important than others.[28]

For this reason, Afrocentricity can have a significant influence on the manner in which African researchers view their identity and interpret their reality from a centred position to overcome the disorientation and de-centredness created by Eurocentric perspectives.

Jackson and Hogg[29] point out that Afrocentricity should not be viewed as a single monolithic theory of knowledge, but rather constitutes a gathering space for multiple theoretical orientations that focus on African agency, culture,

25 Asante, *Afrocentricity: The Theory of Social Change* (revised, expanded ed.), 1.
26 Mazama, "The Afrocentric Paradigm: Contours and Definitions," 387–8.
27 Mazama, "The Afrocentric Paradigm: Contours and Definitions," 388.
28 Molefi Kete Asante, Afrocentricity and Knowledge: Adjusting Our Narrative lenses, 2017, 24.
29 Ronald L. Jackson and Michael A. Hogg (Eds.), *Encyclopaedia of Identity: Afrocentricity* (Thousand Oaks, CA: Sage, 2010), 2.

history, philosophy and society in an effort to reconstruct a global African identity and subjectivity. Hence, within the political climate constructed by European dominance, no one can assume to be a universal subject or claim to be an objective speaker; rather, we are expressions of a culture. Either we speak from our own cultural perspective or we participate in someone else's cultural perspective – none can claim neutrality. Afrocentricity, therefore, boldly articulates the African cultural standpoint and unashamedly insists on African agency informed by African culture and history as the route to confront Eurocentric dominance.

To provide further clarity on what Afrocentricity is, Asante outlines five principal constituents that distinguish Afrocentricity from any other theoretical viewpoint:[30]

- Afrocentricity emphasizes that Africans should have a passionate interest in their own psychological or emotional location, as determined by symbols, motifs, rituals, ceremonies and signs. The African thinker should seek to determine by icon, myth, motifs, symbols, etc., where a text, person or event is located. This literally implies that no phenomenon can be apprehended adequately without locating it first. To understand the African people is to locate them within their own historical and cultural context, defined by psychological time and space. This clearly suggests that no preconceived ideas originating from outside of African lived experiences can provide a proper understanding of Africans. In this context, a Eurocentric scholar is unable to explain African phenomena adequately without wearing the correct lenses. In fact, it is a culturally hegemonic approach to use a Eurocentric world view to navigate an understanding of Africa and its people.
- Afrocentricity calls on scholars to be committed to finding the subject place of Africans in any inquiry, be it political, social, economic, religious or architectural. The researcher must know where he or she stands in the process of research and must prioritize the interests of the African people. Implementing these principles would enable the Afrocentrist to comment on any injustice against, and the inequality and marginalization of, Africans.
- Afrocentricity insists that Africans must guard African cultural elements as historically valid in the context of art, music, education and literature. To defend African cultural elements means that we must study African cultures and be experts in our field of inquiry.
- Afrocentricity celebrates 'centredness' and 'agency' and stimulates commitment to a lexical refinement and reconstruction that eliminates any misperceptions about Africans.

30 Asante 2017, 25.

It must, therefore, be ascertained whether those who make pronouncements on African-related matters are intellectually located to enable them to offer a proper assessment of the issues. Afrocentricity remains a powerful imperative regarding the revision of historical and social sources to revision the collective story of African people. Afrocentricity advocates a re-education of Africans to overcome the negativity that has been imposed on Africans by European scholarship as a way to liberate knowledge from the Eurocentric hegemony.

In addition to the five principles outlined by Asante regarding what constitutes the essence of Afrocentricity, Ama Mazama has articulated four cardinal elements which must inform Afrocentric research,[31] namely its cosmology, epistemology and axiology, and the aesthetics of African people; the research must also be centred in African experiences.

Regarding cosmology, Asante maintains that the place of African culture in the myths, legends, literatures and oratories of African people makes up, at a mythological level, the cosmological issue in the Afrocentric enterprise.[32] The critical task for Afrocentrists is to examine what role African culture plays in, and what it contributes to, Africans' interface with the cosmos. Therefore, the focus of Afrocentricity is holism. This communicates the idea that systems (physical, biological, chemical, social, economic, mental and linguistic) and their properties should be viewed as a whole, not just as a collection of parts. This implies that Afrocentricity rejects reductionism, which is mostly embedded within Eurocentrism, which has not only dismembered the African continent but also Africans' view of life.

The second cardinal element is African epistemology. To question if there is such a thing called an African epistemology is to question the very existence of the people called Africans, but in particular, it is to question their ability to produce any knowledge unique to their circumstances, in line with their life experiences. It is, therefore, impossible to imagine any future for Africans if we assume Africans do not exist. Asante explains that in his use of 'African' as a prefix, he is referring to a 'composite African', not a specific discrete African orientation that would rather mean ethnic identification, such as Yoruba, Zulu and Nubian.[33] Afrocentricity, therefore, affirms the ability of Africans (in this broad sense) to think and be their own agents, using their own knowledge system informed by their composite history and lived experiences.

---

31 Mazama, "The Afrocentric Paradigm: Contours and Definitions," 399.

32 Asante, *Kemet, Afrocentricity, and Knowledge*, 8–9.

33 Molefi Kete Asante, "The Principal Issues in Afrocentric Inquiry," in *African Intellectual Heritage: A Book of Sources*, eds. Molefi Kete Asante and Abu Shardow Abarry (Philadelphia, PA: Temple University Press, 1996), 256.

Senghor suggests that the African mode of cognition is more emotionally laden than purely rational.[34] He maintains that European forms of thought or reasoning rely solely on rationalism; they are analytic and discursive, whereas African reasoning is intuitive. African knowledge therefore emerges from the cooperation of all human faculties and experience, not only reasoning.

The third critical aspect in Afrocentric inquiry, according to Mazama, is an axiological aspect.[35] Axiology, which is also called the theory of value, is the philosophical study of goodness, or value. In an Afrocentric inquiry, axiology concerns that which is deemed tolerable and that which is not tolerable in the context of the African world view. Afrocentrists believe that the practice of research must hold African history and the lived experiences of Africans in the highest esteem. That which articulates the best interest of the African people – particularly, their liberation from all forms of Eurocentric hegemony – should occupy the hearts of the researchers. Hence, the focal point in Afrocentricity is the relocation and re-centring of Africans within their cultural context, as a way to dislodge Western ways of thinking, being and feeling and restore them to the modes that are germane to their cultural perspective. In this context, Mazama argues that without re-centring ourselves to the African cultural context, we remain displaced, and having lost sight of ourselves in the midst of what she describes as European decadence and madness, it becomes increasingly impossible for us to position our lives in a positive and constructive manner.[36]

The last important issue in Afrocentricity relates to aesthetics. According to Asante, aesthetics exists as the leading element of the African response to the arts, whether these are the plastic or performing arts.[37] Welsh-Asante also points out that an understanding of aesthetics facilitates the paradigm for artistic, literary and philosophical criticism and scholarship.[38] In addition, Welsh-Asante maintains that the cultural dynamics of people creates a specific aesthetic complexion.[39] For this reason, African aesthetics plays a critical role in affirming the ability of African people to be innovative and to contribute to building their own societies. African people should, therefore, not merely be seen as objects that must be fashioned into the image and artistic expressions of a European cultural ethos. Rather, they must affirm their right to be their own agents in the multicultural global context.

---

34 Leopold S. Senghor, *On African Socialism*, transl. with an introduction by Mercer Cook (London: Pall Mall Press, [1959] 1964).

35 Mazama, "The Afrocentric Paradigm: Contours and Definitions."

36 Mazama, "The Afrocentric Paradigm: Contours and Definitions," 387–8.

37 Asante, *Kemet, Afrocentricity, and Knowledge*, 11.

38 Kariamu Welsh-Asante, *The African Aesthetic: Keeper of the Traditions* (Westport, CT: Praeger Press, 1994).

39 Welsh-Asante, *The African Aesthetic.*

In line with the five principles articulated by Asante and the four cardinal elements of Afrocentric research articulated by Mazama, the foundational and ultimate goal of Afrocentricity is to expose and resist white racial domination over Africans in all matters of African life and to restore Africans to their cultural centre. Culture remains a central aspect in Asante's analysis, and he defines it as 'shared perceptions, attitudes, and pre-dispositions that allow African people to organize experiences in certain ways'.[40] In Asante's view, 'Afrocentricity should not be understood as the sheer reverse of Eurocentrism as others suppose rather it ought to be understood as a perspective for analysis which privileges African voices without seeking to become a universal perspective just as Eurocentrism has often done'.[41] Chukwuokolo also affirms that Afrocentricity does not violently confront any person or people, but it is a resolute attempt to put the record straight.[42] It is about placing Africans in their proper historical framework, by demanding that the contributions of Africans in all areas of civilization be correctly reflected in world history.

Therefore, Afrocentrists do not seek to impose an African-centred world view on other people or posit that it is the *only* and exclusive framework for legitimate knowledge production. For Afrocentrists, the widely held misconception that human progress emanates only from white people and not the entirety of the human race shrinks the status of non-whites and promotes epistemic racism. Afrocentricity, therefore, seeks to position itself intellectually alongside other knowledges as a valid canon of thought. It calls on Africans to be heedful in scrutinizing all aspects related to their being as a way to dismantle the Eurocentric hegemony over their lives. Afrocentrists, therefore, argue for diversity in philosophical views without hierarchy and call for all cultural centres to be respected.

Historical Roots of Afrocentricity

Afrocentricity was conceptualized and crystallized through the writings of Molefi Kete Asante (its leading theorist), who, in the late 1970s, initiated discussions on the significance of an Afrocentric orientation to data.[43,44] In 1980, Molefi Asante popularized his ideas through the book

40 Asante, *Kemet, Afrocentricity, and Knowledge*, 9.
41 Asante, *Afrocentricity: The Theory of Social Change* (revised, expanded ed.), 5–6.
42 Chukwuokolo, "Afrocentrism or Eurocentrism," 33.
43 Asante, *Afrocentricity* [Online].
44 R. Sentwali Bakari, *Epistemology from an Afrocentric Perspective: Enhancing Black Students' Consciousness through an Afrocentric Way of Knowing. Different Perspectives on Majority Rules* (University of Nebraska-Lincoln, Lincoln, NB, 1997), 20.

titled *Afrocentricity: The Theory of Social Change*, which launched the first full discussion of the concept.[45–48] Asante (born Arthur Lee Smith, Jr), a Professor in the Department of Africology and African American Studies at Temple University (Philadelphia, Pennsylvania), along with other scholars, championed the concept and refined it into a paradigm. Other scholars who have written extensively on Afrocentricity and who worked with Professor Asante include Ama Mazama, Theophile Obenga, C. Tshehloane Keto, Kariamu Welsh-Asante, Abu Abarry and Terry Kershaw. Asante remains the leading scholar of the group.[49,50]

According to Mazama, Afrocentricity as a paradigm should be understood within the context of the PhD programme in the Department of Africology at Temple University in 1988.[51] Mazama explains that the development of this PhD programme was a milestone, not so much because the study programme validated the African experience, but because, for the first time, there was an attempt systematically and consciously to build an army of scholars who would be trained to challenge white supremacy in ways it had never been challenged before.[52]

This theory emerged with an aim to address the life and experiences of people of African descent in America, and by extension on the African continent, and in other diasporas globally. In other words, from its inception, the idea of Afrocentricity sought to transcend the constricted African American context where it was conceptualized into a paradigm and to establish itself as a global idea with the primary objective to address the conditions and lived experiences of Africans in a world dominated by Eurocentrism and racism against Africans. Therefore, Afrocentricity is not a paradigm only for Africans in the diaspora, as others have misrepresented it, but for Africans globally.

---

45 Asante, *Afrocentricity* [Online].

46 Mia Bay, "The Historical Origins of Afrocentrism," *American Studies* 45, no. 4 (2000): 501–12.

47 Midas Chawane, *The Development of Afrocentricity: A Historical Survey. Yesterday & Today*, 2016.

48 Nadezdha Khokholkova, "Afrocentricity: The Evolution of the Theory in the Context of American History," *Social Evolution and History* 15, no. 1 (2016): 113.

49 Khokholkova, "Afrocentricity," 113.

50 Charles C. Verharen, "Molefi Asante and an Afrocentric Curriculum," *Western Journal of Black Studies* 24, no. 4 (2000): 223–38.

51 Mazama, "The Afrocentric Paradigm: Contours and Definitions," 403.

52 Mazama, "The Afrocentric Paradigm: Contours and Definitions."

According to Asante,[53] three intellectual streams are directly linked to the emergence of Afrocentricity, namely Négritude, Diopian historiography and the Kawaida communitarian philosophy as proposed by Maulana Karenga. Although each of these intellectual theories influenced early work in Afrocentricity, the development of Afrocentricity itself must be seen as linked to each of these streams in a different way. Asante acknowledges that from Négritude, Afrocentricity learned that the constituents of resistance to oppression are action and agency, although Asante argues that Négritude did not give us the kind of agency that would reverberate in the work of Afrocentrists.[54] According to Mazama,[55] the leading figures of the Négritude movement, Léopold Senghor, Aime Césaire, and Leon Damas, were struck by the overwhelming colonial nature of French culture, and as university students they became exhausted and enervated by this colonial culture, so they erected defences by projecting what was their own from their ancestors. Mazama maintains that they liberated themselves from European culture when they embraced themselves and saw themselves as beautiful, and something wonderful to behold. However, they were unable to carry this project to completion and often found themselves back in the bosom of whiteness.[56]

Asante (2000) maintains that Afrocentricity is a broader paradigm than Négritude,[57] which depends on *Africanity* much more than on Afrocentricity to wrestle for its place in the discourse of social change. In Asante's view, Africanity focuses primarily on the customs, traditions and traits of the people of Africa and its diaspora.[58] He argues that to be an African by birth does not automatically translate to being Afrocentric; Africanity is a state of being, whereas Afrocentricity is a state of being *conscious* of one's African-ness as it relates to living experiences.[59]

Cheikh Anta Diop's historiography of Africa made a critical contribution to the emergence of Afrocentricity.[60] However, although it is true that Afrocentricity borrows from Diopian historiography in the arena of methodology and historical epistemology, Asante maintains that Afrocentricity

53 Asante, "Afrocentricity and History."

54 Asante, "Afrocentricity and History," 60.

55 Mazama, *The Afrocentric Paradigm.*

56 Mazama, *The Afrocentric Paradigm.*

57 Asante 2000.

58 Asante, *The Afrocentric Idea* (revised, expanded ed.), 19.

59 Asante, "Afrocentricity and History," 60.

60 Cheikh Anta Diop, *The African Origin of Civilization* (New York, NY: Lawrence Hill, 1974); Cheikh Anta Diop, *Civilization or Barbarism: An Authentic Anthropology* (New York, NY: Lawrence Hill, 1981).

is not limited to the subject of history alone.[61] Instead, Afrocentricity is an all-inclusive paradigm that investigates *all* matters affecting African lives from a centred perspective.

Afrocentricity was also influenced by Maulana Karenga's philosophy of Kawaida, which aimed at reorienting corrective action, which included the restoration of cultural values based on African traditions.[62] In Asante's view, Afrocentricity sought to use the Kawaidan critique of culture as a starting point for suggesting African agency in addressing the oppressive environment and how such an environment has influenced African reactions to remedy the situation.[63] The reconstruction of an African value system was thus perceived as an important remedy to reconstruct positivity to confront mental slavery and structural systems designed to oppress. The Kawaidan philosophy provided a base for Afrocentricity's cultural criticism, even though Kawaida focused on ethical aspects, whereas Afrocentricity explores the structural designs that encourage moral decisions.

According to Khokholkova, Afrocentricity did not only develop as an approach but also as a sociopolitical movement. From its very inception, Afrocentric theory was utilitarian, in the sense that it became a guide to action.[64] According to Bay, the adjective 'Afro-centric' was coined by W. E. B. Du Bois in the early 1960s to describe the subject matter of his projected *Encyclopedia Africana*, which was to centre around Africa,[65] but Afrocentricity's contemporary meaning was not defined into a theory of analysis until Asante published his book in the 1980s.[66] Asante suggests that Du Bois prepared the world for Afrocentricity by establishing its foundations.[67] As stated earlier, Asante also explicitly cites Cheikh Anta Diop, the Senegalese historian, as the precursor of Afrocentricity, because he reconstructed African cultural theory with Africa as a subject.[68]

According to Chawane, the fact that Afrocentricity emerged in the United States of America has led some scholars erroneously to assume that it is a theory exclusively for African American scholars.[69] For example, Collins argues that for 'one to become an Afrocentrist, he or she must be located within an African value

61 Asante, "Afrocentricity and History."
62 Asante, "Afrocentricity and History."
63 Asante, "Afrocentricity and History," 61.
64 Khokholkova, "Afrocentricity," 114.
65 Bay, "The Historical Origins of Afrocentrism," 502.
66 Bay, "The Historical Origins of Afrocentrism," 503.
67 Asante, Molefi Kete, *Afrocentricity* (Trenton, NJ: Africa World Press, 1988), 16.
68 Molefi Kete Asante, *The Afrocentric Idea* (revised, expanded ed.), 1988.
69 Chawane, *The Development of Afrocentricity*, 84.

system, thus, any paradigm that seeks to explain the existential socio-cultural circumstances of African people must be centred or located within the African continent'.[70] Mafeje,[71] who also endorses African-centredness, echoes Collins's views, arguing that 'black African Americans are first Americans and second to anything else they choose, like all Americans and irrespective of what they do, black Americans cannot hope to re-appropriate Africa. Any attempt to do so would lead to intellectual confusion and conceptual distortions'. Mafeje is of the view that 'Africa must be studied from within in order to reclaim one's identity'.[72]

However, the view held in this study is that the history of African oppression and colonization did not begin in America, rather it started in Africa; hence, the general history of Africans can never be complete without recognizing the Africans who became the victims of the Transatlantic slave trade and whose descendants form the bulk of the African American segment of the American population today. In addition, there is always a sense of solidarity and a constant search by Africans in the diaspora for a common historical mission, for the elements that bind them together as a group, other than a common history of oppression. To exclude African Americans or Africans in the diaspora from the study of Africans would be an error, in failing to admit that they are Africans taken from Africa in the first place. In this regard, Asante cites Du Bois, who once stated that 'he speaks first and foremost as a son of Africa and calls to Africa, Egypt, and Ethiopia and the need for Afro-Americans to see their thinking, self-understanding, and intellectual efforts to be related to those of Africans'[73] (Asante, 2017:27).

The argument that African Americans cannot claim their status as Africans is merely another attempt by Eurocentric scholars (both white and black) to divide Africans as one group of people with a common origin and common experiences of oppression. European historiography has separated Africans into different groupings as a strategy to disrupt African unity against its oppressive strategies. It is important to note that most scholars agree that the experiences of enslavement and racism directed at Africans in American society created the conditions for the emergence of the Afrocentric theory.[74–76] Verharen agrees that the experiences of slaves

70 Patricia Hill Collins, *Black Feminist Thought* (New York, NY: Routledge, 1991), 206.
71 Mafeje, "Africanity," 69.
72 Mafeje, "Africanity," 67.
73 Asante 2017.
74 Khokholkova, "Afrocentricity."
75 Monteiro-Ferreira, *The Demise of the Inhumane.*
76 Verharen, "Molefi Asante."

in the Middle Passage during the Transatlantic slave trade, the denial of education to slaves once they landed in the Americas and the double cultures of Africanisms and Americanisms stimulated Afro-American hypersensitivity to culture and its relativity.[77] The role of Afrocentricity as a theory is to advance African unity based on African culture and history, with Africans as their own agents and subjects of their historical tale, and not as objects of the European modernization agenda.

The Leitmotifs of Afrocentricity

Afrocentricity as a theory of knowledge proposes that knowledge about Africa and Africans be re-investigated cross-continentally, as a way to subvert the epistemic racism created throughout the history of Eurocentrism and its colonization of the terms of reference. Afrocentricity attempts to address all aspects of African lives, but there are specific topics that are widely covered within Afrocentricity which are considered of critical importance. Chawane outlines some of the interrelated critical key topics including the contribution of ancient Africa to world civilization, a perspective on African history, slavery, colonialism and racism.[78] These topics are discussed below.

Afrocentricity and its perspective on African history and Africa's contributions to ancient civilization

Afrocentricity posits that African history and Africa's contribution to world civilization necessitate a unique perspective on the study of African people, as many of their contributions were intentionally misreported because of racist Eurocentric scholarship. According to Adeleke, the idea of Afrocentric history as narrated by black thinkers developed as a resistance strategy against the negative European tale of African history.[79] This implies that the emergence of Afrocentric historicism emerged as a search by Africans to understand their roots and to narrate their story correctly.

The primary argument advanced by Afrocentrists is that the study of the continent of Africa and its people requires proper research from an African-centred perspective since the achievements and contributions of Africans were deliberately destroyed and twisted by European invaders. Chawane states that Western scholars driven by racism and cultural

77 Verharen, quoted in Chawane, *The Development of Afrocentricity*, 81.

78 Chawane, *The Development of Afrocentricity*, 86.

79 Tunda Adeleke, "Africa and Afrocentric Historicism: A Critique," *Advances in Historical Studies* 4, no. 3 (2015): 202.

arrogance intentionally downplay the achievements made by Africans in Antiquity as a strategy to deny Africans their humanity, thus portraying them as uncivilized humans with no history to tell.[80] In the words of Adeleke, 'the black experience in America and the black experience worldwide has borne the burden of Western history, which is a history of negation'.[81] This historical narrative described Africa as the 'dark continent' and Africans as barbarians and heathens who needed civilization and enlightenment from Europeans. This narration denies people of African ancestry a credible space among civilized beings. For this reason, the colonization of the non-Europeans was justified as a 'civilizing' and 'Christianizing' mission to forestall criticism of the actions of the Europeans who invaded Africa.

Perspectives on Africa's contribution to human civilization vary depending on who writes on African history and for what purpose. Most European historians deliberately minimized the contributions made by Africans, while Afrocentric writers and historians credited black civilization in Egypt with many cultural advances. Thus, the rewriting of African history by black intellectuals was part of black resistance against racist European scholarship, which deliberately downplayed Africa's contribution to world civilization. Generations of black intellectuals since the nineteenth century have undertaken this struggle for historical legitimation.[82,83] Afrocentric scholars rebelled epistemically against false European narratives of Africa by rewriting African history with the objective of correcting these historical injustices. For example, Nwala (cited in Chukwuokolo) notes that

> African achievements in science and philosophy were appropriated as European achievements. Thus, we read about such African philosophers like St. Augustine, Origen, Philo, Plontinus, Porphyry, and many others as part of Western intellectual tradition and achievement. The great achievements of Egyptian thought were largely appropriated as European achievements.[84]

Eurocentric bias was a strategy to elevate Europe as the centre of world history, thus downplaying the civilizations and the technological and

---

80 Chawane, *The Development of Afrocentricity*, 86.

81 Adeleke, "Africa and Afrocentric Historicism," 200.

82 John Ernest, *Liberation Historiography: African American Writers and the Challenge of History, 1794–1861* (Chapel Hill, NC: University of North Carolina Press, 2004).

83 Stephen G. Hall, *A Faithful Account of the Race: African American Historical Writing in 19th Century America* (Chapel Hill, NC: University of North Carolina Press, 2009).

84 Quoted in Chukwuokolo, "Afrocentrism or Eurocentrism," 31.

intellectual achievements of those outside of Europe, in particular Africans. It is in this context that Asante (2017) emphasizes that the Eurocentric argument that the ancient Egyptians were not black Africans and that the Great Zimbabwean walls and the pyramids were not built by Africans need to be challenged.[85] He adds that Africa's influence on ancient Greece (considered Europe's oldest civilization) was enormous, in art, geometry, medicine, mathematics, architecture, politics, astronomy and religion (Asante, 2017).[86] However, racist Eurocentric scholarship has continued to undermine and discredit Africa as a place of barbarism with no history.

One of the most notorious instances of Eurocentric racism by scholars in the narrative of African history was postulated in G. W. F. Hegel's series of lectures in the first half of the nineteenth century in his *Philosophy of History*. Hegel divided Africa into three regions: North Africa, Egypt and 'Africa proper'.[87] Hegel's views were grounded on the idea of European racial superiority, as he believed that nothing good could come from black Africans. His artificial division of Africa was aimed at cementing the idea that black Africans were nothing but uncivilized barbarians devoid of culture and history and had nothing to offer. Historians of that period tended to invalidate African people in order to justify the idea that Africans should be civilized and enlightened into the image of a European man as a way to redeem them from their barbarism. Hume had earlier framed a similar racist attack on black Africans:

> I am apt to suspect the Negroes and in general all other species of men to be naturally inferior to the whites. There never was a civilized nation of any other complexion than white, nor even any individual eminent in either action or speculation. No ingenious manufactures amongst them, no arts, no sciences.[88]

This malicious web of intellectual bias and racist posturing continued to inform how Europeans looked down on Africans and other non-European people. For this reason, Afrocentrists aim to reclaim Africa and the civilizational achievements of its people in order to combat Eurocentric misrepresentations.

---

85 Asante 2017.

86 Asante 2017.

87 Georg Wilhelm Friedrich Hegel, *The Philosophy of History*, transl. J. Sibree (New York: Dover, 1956).

88 David Hume, "Of National Characters," in *Essays, Moral, Political and Literary* (Harmondsworth: Penguin, [1748] 1969), 208.

Chukwuokolo suggests that the biases of the Eurocentric intellectual atmosphere were conducive to Europeans' subtly (and often not so subtly) manipulating Africans' consciousness to view their realities from the European perspective in all spheres, be it social, political, developmental, technological or scientific.[89] Hence, the primary objective of Afrocentrists is to rally African scholars and educators to rewrite the whole landscape of African history to ensure the preservation of African heritage, culture and contributions to world civilization. Asante makes this clear:

> [T]he fact of the matter is that the history of Africa written by European scholars discounts and twists the substantial evidence of African influence on Greece. In particular, to bring to light that ancient Egypt was before ancient Greece as ancient Greece was before Rome, in this way the Greeks are left in their place and the Egyptians are respected for their achievements, without seeking to relegate them to the junior status.[90]

The goal of Afrocentricity is, therefore, to reaffirm Africa as a place of greatness that has contributed immensely to world civilization in order to instil a victorious consciousness to overthrow Eurocentric misrepresentations of world history and to set the record straight.

The re-narration of African history must reopen discussions on everything from race theory to ancient civilizations, colonial and post-colonial, African and European personalities, and dislocation in the writing of African authors.[91]

Afrocentricity's perspective on racism, slavery and colonialism

Afrocentrists maintain that the subject of race and racism must be tackled urgently because it has contributed to a falsified understanding of Africa and its people. Although the construct of race is more recent, Afrocentrists argue that a racist line of thought has its roots as far back as the fifteenth century.[92] Olusoga demonstrates that from the fifteenth century to date – the entire period during which Europeans and Africans have been connected through trade, empire and migration, both forced and voluntary – Europe has viewed

89 Chukwuokolo, "Afrocentrism or Eurocentrism," 31.

90 Asante, *Afrocentricity* [Online], 1–2.

91 Asante, *An Afrocentric Manifesto: Toward an African Renaissance.*

92 Molefi Kete Asante, *Facing South to Africa.*

the people of Africa through the distorting lens of racism and racial theory.[93] During the era of colonialism and Transatlantic slave trade, the idea of race was invented as a strategy to oppress and exterminate Africans. Asante highlights that in the Netherlands, around the same era in which David Hume was writing, Peter Campier compared facial and skull measurements of black people and monkeys and developed a hierarchy in which he said that the Greek statuary was the highest form and the lowest was the Negro.[94] During the late eighteenth century, at the University of Gottingen, Wilhelm and Alexander von Humboldt began to develop the racial hierarchical theories that would shape European thought into the next centuries and cause Africans to question themselves.[95] The European colonialists recruited historians, ethnographers, clergymen and scientists to do the ignoble job of degrading Africans into the 'zone of non-human beings'.[96]

Chawane complains that the European colonizers projected themselves as the liberators and saviours of the African savages with the primary objective of freeing them from their barbarism and primitive state into the civilized trajectory of the European man.[97] They downplayed the fact that they were raping the people and the land, and robbing them of their possessions, enriching themselves. Asante emphasizes that the colonial masters claimed to be obeying the precepts of 'universal reason' ; anything contrary to their way of thinking was an act of irrationality and backwardness.[98] They cared little about understanding African culture and modes of production, and imposed their own, which amounts to a malicious assault that rendered Africans the objects of colonial oppression. For this reason, European colonization not only fractured the African physical environment but extended itself to unleashing cultural disintegration aimed at destroying African lives. Ekeh rightly argues that

> [...] colonialism as a process cannot be simplistically understood as an event of conquest and rule of Africa by Europeans. Rather, it must be viewed as a systemic social movement of epochal dimensions whose enduring consequences outlives the end of direct colonialism.[99]

---

93 David Olusoga, "The Roots of European Racism Lie in the Slave Trade, Colonialism – and Edward Long," *The Guardian*, 8 Sept. 2015.

94 Asante, *Afrocentricity: The Theory of Social Change.*

95 Asante, *Afrocentricity: The Theory of Social Change.*

96 Chukwuokolo, Afrocentrism or Eurocentrism, 172.

97 Chawane, *The Development of Afrocentricity*, 87.

98 Molefi Kete Asante, "Afrocentricity and Knowledge: Adjusting the Narrative Lens," *The Thinker Magazine* 74 (2017): 24–26.

99 Peter Ekeh, cited in Ndlovu-Gatsheni 2017, p. 2.

Essentially, the success of the colonial enterprise relied not just on the physical subjugation of Africans and their continent but the colonization of the mind and the fostering of a slave mentality among Africans. Chawane clearly articulates this as follows: 'Colonisation of the mind of Africans could not succeed without taking away the language and names of the ruled and replacing them with those of the ruler.'[100]

The scramble for Africa reached its highest point in the 1884/85 Berlin Conference, mapping out the continent, and resulting in Africans losing their lands and being reduced to nonentities and to an unwanted, albeit human-like species. This conference introduced and defined the rules of the partition of Africa among 14 European nations without any regard for the lives of African people. According to Asante, what emerged from this meeting of self-confident imperial conferees were three important doctrines that would govern European political and military policies towards Africa for more than a century and beyond:

> The doctrine of the spheres of influence by which Europe established its right to control the African coastline. The doctrine of effective occupation by which Europe established the idea that it could occupy an entire country by controlling the commerce along the coast. Lastly, the doctrine of European protection of its agents, especially missionaries, explorers, and scientists who exploited the African people's resources.[101]

Despite the attempts by Europeans to impose total control on the continent, Africans resisted and continue to resist, just as in the early days of European invasion beginning from the late fifteenth century. Ndlovu-Gatsheni[102] and Asante[103] attest that African people organized their resistance against European domination by deploying Pan-Africanism and African nationalism as strategies for projecting their agency to contest the immanent logic of their dehumanization, manifested through the slave trade, imperialism and colonialism. This point is addressed in detail in Chapter 6.

---

100 Chawane, *The Development of Afrocentricity*, 89.

101 Asante, *Afrocentricity* [Online], 1–2.

102 Sabelo J. Ndlovu-Gatsheni, "The Entrapment of Africa within the Global Colonial Matrices of Power: Eurocentrism, Coloniality, and Deimperialization in the Twenty-First Century," *Journal of Developing Societies* 29, no. 4 (2013): 331–53.

103 Asante, *Afrocentricity* [Online].

Afrocentricity and Its Critics

Afrocentricity has provoked much controversy and has been harshly attacked by many Eurocentric scholars, both black and white. These critics have labelled it a pseudohistory, a reactive posture and a mere therapeutic scholarship of those who are desperate to heal the wounds of the past, but display an unwillingness to forgive the historical past.[104] These critics include Adeleke,[105] Early, Moses and Lefkowitz,[106,107] Richburg,[108] Shavit,[109] Walker,[110] Owens[111] and many more. The critical arguments advanced by these scholars relate to the three primary objectives that they argue to be the main points in Afrocentricity: establishing the antiquity of history and civilization in Africa; affirming the influence of Egyptian civilization on ancient Greece, and by extension, the proclamation of Africa's superiority over European civilization; and finally, proclaiming the 'universality' of the African world view.[112]

In the first chapter of his book, *History in Black: African Americans in Search of Their Past*, Shavit describes Afrocentrism as the historical account of black people, stating that it constitutes articles of faith, a gospel, a collective and personal revelation, but also a scientific (pseudo-scientific) historical dogma, and a mass project of rewriting human history.[113] He recognizes that the aim of the Afrocentric movement and its theorization is an attempt to provide a revised history of the past, one in which Africans are the founders and architects of all cultures and the main agents of change worldwide. However, Shavit claims that Afrocentrism offers only an imaginary monolithic Afrocentric universal history in an attempt to construct a black identity.[114]

---

104 Yaacov Shavit, *History in Black: African-Americans in Search of an Ancient Past* (London: Frank Cass, 2001).

105 Adeleke, "Africa and Afrocentric Historicism."

106 Gerald Early, Wilson. J. Moses, and Mary R. Lefkowitz, "Symposium: Historical Roots of Afrocentrism," *Academic Questions*, 7, no. 2 (1994): 44–54.

107 Mary R. Lefkowitz, *Not out of Africa: How Afrocentrism Became an Excuse to Teach Myth as History* (New York, NY: Basic Books, 1996).

108 Keith B. Richburg, *Out of America: A Black Man Confronts Africa* (New York, NY: Basic Books, 1996).

109 Shavit, *History in Black.*

110 Clarence E. Walker, *Why We Can't Go Home Again: An Argument about Afrocentrism* (New York, NY: Oxford University Press, 2001).

111 Michael Eric Owens, *Yes, I Am Who I Am: A New Philosophy of Black Identity* (Tulsa, OK: Yorkshire Publishing, 2009).

112 Adeleke, "Africa and Afrocentric Historicism," 205.

113 Shavit, *History in Black.*

114 Shavit, *History in Black.*

Applying a similar line of argument, Moses, in the joint essay by Early et al., also criticizes Afrocentrism as a form of utopian or millenarian movement which romanticizes the African past.[115] He compares Afrocentrists with Christian evangelists who have undergone the kind of charismatic spiritual experience that the African American psychologist William R. Cross has labelled 'the Negro to Black Conversion Experience'. Moses contemptuously attacks the Afrocentrists by suggesting that those who 'convert' to Afrocentrism often change their names as a sign that they have put off the old man and put on the new man.[116] He believes that Afrocentrists are fundamentalists who do not argue in a scholarly manner and claims that Afrocentricity is not an intellectual movement but a secular religion, which assumes itself to hold the absolute truth. To him, Afrocentrism is not a political ideology – rather it is a utopian evangelical cult that is anti-intellectual.[117]

Lefkowitz is another Eurocentric scholar who criticizes the historical claims of Afrocentricity that Egyptians were the founders of Greek civilization. Lefkowitz, in the same joint essay, criticizes the claims made by Afrocentrists,[118] and in particular, by George G. M. James in his book, *Stolen Legacy*,[119] that the Greeks were not the authors of Greek philosophy, but that black people of North Africa, the Egyptians, were. Lefkowitz dismisses such views as untrue and sensationalist, as not supported by scholarly evidence.[120] Lefkowitz lambasts the theory of *Stolen Legacy* for its lack of evidence and as mere false proclamations.[121] She claims that if the great Greek philosophers had stolen their ideas from Egyptians, as James[122] posits, she would expect evidence of texts showing frequent verbal parallels. However, as it is, James only highlights some generalized similarities between Egyptian religious ideas and Greek theories and fails to prove them by producing written evidence, according to Lefkowitz.[123] She closes her argument by suggesting that such misinformation entitles *Stolen Legacy* to a place on the shelf with other hate literature, as a mere influential mythology in recent history.

---

115 Early et al., "Symposium," 46.
116 Early et al., "Symposium," 46.
117 Early et al., "Symposium," 46.
118 Early et al., "Symposium," 51.
119 George G. M. James, *Stolen Legacy* (New York, NY: Classic House Books, [1954] 2009).
120 Early et al., "Symposium."
121 Early et al., "Symposium."
122 James, *Stolen Legacy*.
123 Early et al., "Symposium," 53.

Adeleke is also among the scholars who have criticized Afrocentricity.[124] He maintains that Afrocentric historicism's framing of Africa is nothing but the sheer reverse of Eurocentric racist history, replacing it with the black racist historiography. He argues that Afrocentric historicism constitutes a fundamentalist and absolutist discourse that has repositioned Africa in the 'universalist' edifice from which Afrocentric scholars have dislodged Europe.[125] This attempt by Afrocentric scholars represents the basis of what Shavit decries as Afrocentric Greek dependency theory.[126]

The critics of Afrocentricity argue that its logic is simplistic. Shavit argues that if ancient Greece was the fountain of Western culture, and if it could be proven that Greek culture was heavily influenced by Egypt, it seems reasonable to depict Western civilization as a product of non-Whites, referring to Africans in particular.[127] It would then be this view that influenced Afrocentric scholars to invoke the 'stolen legacy theory' as articulated by James.[128] From this view, Afrocentric scholars then merely characterize Western civilization as nothing but the product of 'stolen' ancient Egyptian legacies.

Another critical point raised by the critics of Afrocentricity relates to the Afrocentric idea of 'Pan-Africanism and identity paradigm'. In the opinion of W. D. Wright, the Afrocentric 'Pan-African' construction of identity establishes no boundaries separating continental Africa and the black diaspora, and merely presents one global world idealism.[129] Such critics ignore the view that black Americans and continental Africans have always been drawn together by shared historical and cultural experiences despite centuries of exposure to, and acculturation in, Western values – such a view is argued to be untrue and is decried as a myth that must be challenged.[130] Adeleke maintains that the 'Pan-African' identity paradigm as preached by Afrocentric scholars contradicts Du Bois's duality theory.[131] W. E. B. Du Bois articulated his view of 'double-consciousness' as follows:

> It is a peculiar sensation, this double-consciousness, this sense of always looking at oneself through the eyes of the others, of measuring one's soul; by the tape of a world that looks on in amused contempt

124 Adeleke, "Africa and Afrocentric Historicism," 204–6.

125 Adeleke, "Africa and Afrocentric Historicism," 206.

126 Shavit, *History in Black*, 30.

127 Shavit, *History in Black*.

128 James, *Stolen Legacy*.

129 Cited in Adeleke, "Africa and Afrocentric Historicism," 207.

130 Adeleke, "Africa and Afrocentric Historicism."

131 Adeleke, "Africa and Afrocentric Historicism."

> and pity. One ever feels his twoness- an American, a Negro; two souls, two thoughts, two unreconciled strivings; two warring ideals in one dark body, whose dogged strength alone keeps it from being torn asunder.[132]

Adeleke argues that while acknowledging the American experience, Afrocentric scholars seek to delegitimize its identitarian significance. He maintains that Afrocentricity builds a flawed historical account, which simply suggests that African Americans came out of slavery and the American experience with their African identity intact.[133] Therefore, according to Adeleke, the portrayal of black Americans (African Americans) and Africans (continental) as one people unified by cultural attributes and historical experiences, as pertains to the argument advanced by Afrocentrists, is theoretically and practically flawed.[134] According to Richburg[135] and Owens,[136] the 'Pan-African' idea raised by Afrocentric scholars and their common African heritage romanticizes history. Both these scholars represent what Adeleke has termed the 'slavocentric' perspective,[137] as they reject any commonality between black Americans and continental Africans; in their view, black Americans today have nothing to do with Africa.

Moreover, with regard to the idea of 'continental unity' among Africans, Shavit suggests that Africa is not as homogeneous as Afrocentricity would like us to believe, but that the continent has a multiplicity of languages, genetic variants and profound religious differences. He, therefore, argues that Afrocentricity and its historical projections are just an attempt to build a nation of blacks on false historical grounds and should be rejected.[138]

Afrocentricity's Response to Its Critics

According to Keita, the vast academic corporate pursuit of uniformity, rooted in the tradition of the assertive Euro-American reach for hegemony in thought, inevitably leads to confrontations between Afrocentrists and those who would

132 W. E. B. Du Bois, *The Souls of Black Folk: Essays and Sketches* (Chicago, IL: Lawrence Hill, 1903), 30. In citing Du Bois, I respect the fact that Du Bois preferred to use the initials rather than his full names.

133 Adeleke, "Africa and Afrocentric Historicism," 208.

134 Adeleke, "Africa and Afrocentric Historicism."

135 Richburg, *Out of America*, xiv.

136 Owens, *Yes, I Am Who I Am*, 128.

137 Adeleke, "Africa and Afrocentric Historicism," 208.

138 Shavit, *History in Black.*

like to subsume all new ideas under some or other form of Eurocentrism.[139] As a strategy to maintain their intellectual hegemony over their colonial subjects, Eurocentric scholars have made it their priority to shoot down any idea that seeks to challenge the status quo. Responding to the critics of Afrocentricity, Asante argues that 'it has become plain to see that some scholars are nervous about the possibility of a perspective on data, that is, a locative thesis, which does not adapt to the overarching ideas of a European hegemony'.[140] Asante further notes that 'everyone now has something to say and normally what they have to say is critical of the fact that Afrocentricity appears "outside" the mainstream'.[141] Afrocentricity is 'outside' because it traces its genealogy from the African ideas and African authors; it is not Eurocentric in its analysis, for if it were, it would mean Europe would be assaulting its own patriarchy and a sense of superiority in language, content and structure.

One of the emerging Afrocentric scholars, Gwekwerere, in affirming Asante's words, rightly reminds us that 'European scholars who have made it their business to indict the Afrocentric historicism, culture and conception of reality are products of culture and a history that stand unrivalled in vilifying African people'.[142]

Responding to his critics, both white and black, Asante argues that Afrocentricity should not be confused with 'Afrocentrism', as many scholars do.[143] He argues that the opponents of Afrocentricity first used the term 'Afrocentrism': 'Their aim was to assign religious signification to the idea of African-centredness, but the term has come to refer to a broad cultural movement of the late 20th century and its philosophical, political, and artistic ideas, which provide the basis for the musical, sartorial, and aesthetic dimensions of the African personality.'[144] Moreover, Afrocentricity, as I have stated earlier, is a theory of agency: the idea that African people must be viewed as agents rather than as spectators to historical revolution and change. Therefore, Asante argues that Afrocentricity precedes Afrocentrism, that is, it is older as a term in the intellectual discourse.[145] Lewis R. Gordon affirms Asante's position by arguing that

---

139 Maghan Keita, *Race and the Writing of History: Riddling the Sphinx* (New York, NY: Oxford University Press, 2000).

140 Asante, *An Afrocentric Manifesto: Toward an African Renaissance*, 3.

141 Asante, *An Afrocentric Manifesto: Toward an African Renaissance*, 3.

142 Tavengwa Gwekwerere, "From Nat Turner to Molefi Asante: Reading the European Intellectual Indictment of the Afrocentric Conception of Reality," *Journal of Black Studies* 41, no. 1 (2010): 120.

143 Asante, "Afrocentricity and History," 52.

144 Asante, "Afrocentricity and History," 52.

145 Asante, "Afrocentricity and History."

> [...] the confusion emerges from the fact that proponents of Afrocentricity refer to themselves as Afrocentric, which unfortunately means that their work is mistaken for, as many of them have protested, Afrocentrism, which, they further argue, presents itself as a centrism along with Eurocentrism but with a black face.[146]

This misnaming of Afrocentricity as Afrocentrism clearly reflects an attempt to misdirect those who have not immersed themselves in the essence of what Afrocentricity really constitutes, and this is indicative of ongoing ideological warfare to ensure the continuation of the subjugation of African people as objects of analysis, thus discouraging them from being agents in their own history.

Gwekwerere argues that 'the Eurocentric prerogative to subvert Afrocentricity is born out of the struggle for European survival and is inspired by the desire to keep the world misinformed in order that Europeans may escape their inferiority and crimes committed in history'.[147] As a strategy to evade criticism, these scholars accuse Afrocentricity of what they themselves are guilty of, which is to use political propaganda and present it as scholarly work to deny Africans a voice and agency. As a result, the systematic analysis of scholarly research and theory is watered down as politicians pose as academics to discredit published scholarly work for the sake of political expediency.

Hilliard argues that 'much of the public's understanding of Afrocentricity heavily relies on journalists, rather than on the published research from Afrocentric scholars'.[148] Alkebulan mentions, for example, the media's misrepresentations of Afrocentricity:[149] the media have constructed Lefkowitz's book *Not Out of Africa*[150] as a definitive criticism of Afrocentrism (again mistaken for Afrocentricity). Along with Lefkowitz, others, including Adeleke,[151] Owens,[152] Richburg,[153] Shavit[154] and many more critics, represent a rejection of Afrocentricity without accepting the facts of history regarding African negation and do not see the significance of African agency.

---

146 Lewis R. Gordon, *An Introduction to Africana Philosophy* (New York, NY: Cambridge University Press, 2008), 106.

147 Gwekwerere, "From Nat Turner," 5.

148 Asa G. Hilliard, III, "Bridging Maat, Destroying Isfet: The African and African Diasporian Presence in the Study of Ancient Kmt," in *Egypt: Child of Africa*, edited by Ivan van Sertima, New Brunswick, NJ: Transaction Publishers, 1995, 130.

149 Alkebulan, Adisa A., "Defending the Paradigm," *Journal of Black Studies*, 37, no. 3 (2007): 422.

150 Lefkowitz, *Not Out of Africa.*

151 Adeleke, "Africa and Afrocentric Historicism."

152 Owens, *Yes, I Am Who I Am.*

153 Richburg, *Out of America.*

154 Shavit, *History in Black.*

Asante writes in *The Painful Demise of Eurocentrism: An Afrocentric Response to Critics* in response to Lefkowitz: 'The aim of Professor Lefkowitz is to support the unsupportable idea of a miraculous Greece and thus to enhance a white supremacist myth of the ancient world.'[155] The primary motive of the book is, therefore, to further discredit Africans as incapable beings without the ability to represent themselves. This is done as a political strategy to deny African agency and to cement Eurocentric lies regarding Africans' contributions to world civilization.

The proponents of Afrocentricity have classified the three types of opponents of Afrocentricity and their reasons for opposing it: Capitulationists, Europeanized Loyalists and Maskers.[156] Capitulationists condemn Afrocentricity because they are uncomfortable with themselves and do not believe that Africans should be considered agents. They include, among black scholars, Appiah, Crouch,[157] Adeleke, Richburg and Owens. According to Chawane, the functioning element for these critics is self-hatred, accompanied by the belief that these African critics are really nothing but whites in a black skin.[158] Their rejection of Afrocentricity is tied to their rejection of themselves. Therefore, they seek affirmation from whites because of their lack of grounding in their own historical consciousness. Moreover, the Capitulationists aspire to universalism without references to their particular experiences. For them, any emphasis on particular perspectives and experiences suggests separatism, and separatism suggests hostility.[159] The second type, the Europeanized Loyalists, includes many Marxists and integrationists such as Lefkowitz, Early, Moses, Wilson and Shavit, who are staunch critics of Afrocentricity. These critics oppose the Afrocentric idea because they have immersed themselves in an alien canon of knowledge without knowing African history.[160] The last type, the Maskers, is critics who are ashamed of Afrocentricity and therefore deliberately do all they can to conceal their ideological framework and identity, thus posing as universalists. Their tragedy is that they seek to please their masters, so they attack Afrocentricity to prove to whites that they are like them, for fear that they may lose their careers.[161]

155 Molefi Kete Asante, *The Painful Demise of Eurocentrism: An Afrocentric Response to Critics* (Trenton, NJ: Africa World Press, 1999), 51.

156 Chawane, *The Development of Afrocentricity*.

157 Stanley Crouch, "The Afrocentric Hustle," *Journal of Blacks in Higher Education* Winter (1995): 77–82.

158 Chawane, *The Development of Afrocentricity*.

159 Chawane, *The Development of Afrocentricity*.

160 Chawane, *The Development of Afrocentricity*, 97.

161 Asante, "Afrocentricity and Knowledge."

Chapter 3

CRITIQUE OF EUROCENTRISM AND A MAPPING OF AFRICAN DEVELOPMENT INITIATIVES

For Africa as a continent and its people to experience freedom from Western intellectual bondage, the conceptual framing of African development discourse(s) must be re-grounded within African knowledge systems, values, history and culture, through African agency. Such a shift in thinking will enable Africans to participate actively in shaping their own development as agents, rather than merely existing as objects of the European development story. The colonization of Africa by Europeans has framed Africans as people without any history or knowledge of their own to improve the quality of their own lives. As I have already shown, this view of Africans, held by many European scholars, was used to justify the colonization of both Africa as a continent and its people. As a result, Africa's future development was also placed in the hands of Europeans, who were presented as a perfect model of how development was imagined. Anything that seemed to differ from this view was regarded as a form of backwardness. The idea and practice of development in Africa after World War II (from 1945 onwards) was a continuation of the same colonial pattern of undermining African people's capacity to solve their challenges.

Eurocentrism in Development Studies: From Modernization to Neoliberalism

The fundamental challenge facing Development Studies is how the subject can transcend the limitations created by Western epistemology and open the path for alternative development visions. According to Pieterse,[1] Eurocentrism as a guiding intellectual paradigm has long served the agenda of imperial

1 Jan Nederveen Pieterse, "Dilemmas of Development Discourse: The Crisis of Developmentalism and the Comparative Method," *Development and Change*, 22 (1991): 8.

management of societies labelled part of the 'Third World'. In this regard, Ndlovu-Gatsheni raises the following fundamental question: 'What does development mean for a people struggling to emerge and free themselves from the inimical legacies of enslavement, colonialism, imperialism, apartheid, neocolonialism, underdevelopment as well as the imposition of the Washington Consensus and neoliberalism?'[2] In this context, it is important to interrogate the epistemological foundation that informs the nature and structure of development as a discourse in the Global South, and in Africa in particular. The main challenge facing Development Studies in Africa has been the fact that it is a derivative of Western epistemologies and that it is informed by Western experiences and a Western agenda. Therefore, African scholars face the challenge of decolonizing development theory itself to enable contextual relevance.

Brohman argues that 'Western-centric concepts and research methodologies are infused with a false idea of 'universalism' that serves to legitimize their application in diverse Global South nations'.[3] The Eurocentric ideological bias in Development Studies is thus a manifestation of the epistemic racism embedded in the discourse, which has resulted in the exclusion of the non-Western societies in general, and of Africa in particular, from contributing to the body of knowledge relating to their own development. This has happened despite the fact that archaeological evidence has confirmed Africa to have been the cradle of humankind.[4]

African scholars such as Peter Ekeh[5] prefer to use the common term 'colonialism' to highlight the structural straitjacket within which Africa finds itself and the paradigm of difference it has entrenched.[6] Ekeh argues that colonialism cannot be analysed merely as an event of conquest of and rule over Africa by Europeans.[7] Instead, it must be understood as a process that involves a series of events whose enduring consequences have outlived the end of direct colonial administration by European colonizers from competing European nations. The effect of their control endures, even after the political decolonization of the continent. Neocolonial links have ensured that post-colonial governments continue to be subservient to the European agenda of domination.

2 Ndlovu-Gatsheni, "The African Idea of Development," 1.
3 Brohman, "Universalism, Eurocentrism," 128.
4 Ndlovu-Gatsheni, "The Entrapment of Africa," 332.
5 Ekeh, *Colonialism and Social Structure.*
6 Cited in Ndlovu-Gatsheni, "The African Idea of Development," 2.
7 Ekeh, *Colonialism and Social Structure.*

Many post-development scholars, such as Escobar[8] and Esteva and Prakash,[9] have analysed the idea of development as imperialistic and colonial in character. They dismiss the concept as a hegemonic tool used to define the people of the Global South, including African people, as objects of the Euro-North American power structure. In the post-independence era, Africa still has to redefine itself within the colonial framework that denied the continent and its people an avenue to reframe and define development based on its own terms; the continent and its people continue to exist as the periphery constructed by Europe, which imagines itself as the centre of the 'universe'. Escobar's analysis of the axes of development[10] clarifies the relations that shape thinking about development:

> I propose to speak of development as [a] historically singular experience, the creation of the domain of thought and action, by analyzing the characteristics and interrelations of the three axes that define it: the *forms of knowledge* that refer to it and through which it comes into being and is elaborated into objects, concepts, theories, and the like; the *system of power* that regulates its practice; and the *forms of subjectivity* fostered by this discourse, those through which people come to recognise themselves as developed or underdeveloped.[11]

Along similar lines, Ndlovu-Gatsheni points out that development as a construct and practice in the Global South, and in Africa in particular, has not yet been decolonized from epistemic colonial entanglements.[12] Thus, Africa remains a product of worldwide imperialist schemes and their mechanisms of subjugation, which masquerade as liberatory, while in reality serving to perpetuate the colonial order.

Coloniality, in other words, the enduring negative experiences emanating from the process of colonization, continues to shape political governance and the development agenda of post-colonial nation-states in Africa. Hence, Ferguson posits that development as a colonially inspired discourse is not innocent of power and cannot be understood outside of the current global

8 Escobar, *Encountering Development.*

9 Gustavo Esteva and Madhu Suri Prakash, "Beyond Development, What?" *Development in Practice* 8, no. 3 (1998): 280–96.

10 Escobar, *Encountering Development.*

11 Escobar, *Encountering Development,* 10, my emphases.

12 Ndlovu-Gatsheni, Sabelo J., *Coloniality of Power,* 3.

colonial matrices of power dynamics.[13] It is part of what Ferguson terms the 'anti-politics machine'.[14] For this reason, to solve the development impasse in Africa, we must understand the global structuring processes that have shaped the context that informs the very notion of development itself, because the idea of development has long been mobilized by colonial European empires in the context of the history of African dismemberment through colonization enterprises. The entanglement of development as a field of study in the Euro-North American modernization project has the effect that the Global South in general and Africa in particular remain constrained in reimagining a development trajectory on their own terms. In order to unsettle the dominant Eurocentric articulation of development, it is thus necessary to understand how development has been, and continues to be, defined from a Eurocentric perspective.

Amin highlights the epistemic implications of Eurocentrism and coloniality in African conceptions of development, arguing that there is no 'implementation of the principle of auto-centric development' in Africa that is free from the economic rationality of conventional economics.[15] Ndlovu-Gatsheni argues that the ideas of conventional economics, just like all other understandings of the world cascading from Europe and North America, are local European notions that have been universalized.[16] These ideas are rooted in the European canon of thought and are colonial when applied in the African context without allowing African knowledge systems to become a guiding framework in the understanding of economics and development.

In the words of Dussel (1993:65), the idea of enlightenment (also modernity) is, in fact, a European phenomenon, but one constituted in a dialectical relation with the non-European other that is its ultimate content.[17] 'Enlightenment' on Eurocentric terms occurs when Europe affirms itself as the 'centre' of a world history that it inaugurates; the 'periphery' that surrounds this centre is consequently part of its self-definition. Modernity, according to Amin, projects the idea that human beings armed with secular thought and science, individually and collectively, can and must make their history.[18] The tragedy

---

13 James Ferguson, *The Anti-Politics Machine: "Development," Depoliticization, and Bureaucratic Power in Lesotho* (Cambridge: Cambridge University Press, 1990).

14 Ferguson, *The Anti-Politics Machine.*

15 Samir Amin, *Maldevelopment: Anatomy of a Global Failure* (Tokyo and London: United Nations University Press and Zed Books, 1990), 58.

16 Ndlovu-Gatsheni, "The African Idea of Development," 2.

17 Dussel, 65.

18 Amin, *Eurocentrism: Modernity, Religion, and Democracy*, 13.

is that Europe, while asserting itself as the centre, simultaneously denies non-Europeans, and Africans in particular, the right to make and define their own history. Thus, the colonial conception of development remains entrapped within Eurocentrism as a guiding frame of thought that elevates the European view of what progress and civilization entail.

This view demands that the Global South and Africa be moulded into the image of Europe and replicate the historical processes by which Europe came to be the centre of the world. Eurocentrism has thus created the impression of the world as one under Western values and is dismissive of non-Western alternative worldviews. Eurocentrism therefore promotes 'unicentricity', thus denying Africans the right to map out their own development trajectory, informed by African knowledge and understanding of the world, entrenched in its own history and cultural practices. According to Davies, 'unicentricity' (also called One-Centeredness) is a logic that demands a single centre (intellectual, economic, political, cultural and geographic) from which all emanates.[19] In 'unicentricity', the logic of the core and periphery functions to centre some experiences and marginalize others. Thus, Eurocentrism is the basis of dominance and control because it positions Europe and North America in its relations with other countries in terms of competition, hierarchies and subordination, as a strategy to maximize the gains for those countries' Euro-North American counterparts.

For these reasons, the development discourse within the Eurocentric narrative needs to be decolonized and re-articulated from African perspectives to democratize knowledge and liberate the oppressed to speak from their own centres. Therefore, the idea of development rooted in Western experiences should not be projected as a universal model of development because it has long been used as the instrument of conquest to reduce others as peripheral to the West, which falsely assumes the centre stage. It follows a logic according to which non-Europeans can only be said to be progressive if they accept the European cultural ethos and replicate European historical experiences as the sole trajectory towards their development. This implies that outside of Europe (and since the start of the twentieth century, North America) there is no self-initiated development, but mere primitivism and backwardness, which – so the narrative runs – can be overcome by embracing the injunctions of Europe as the epitome of enlightenment.

19 Carole Boyce Davies, "Beyond Unicentricity: Transcultural Black Presences," *Research in African Literatures* 30, no. 2 (1999): 96.

The Post–World War II Development Project and Its Implications for Africa

Post-Enlightenment conceptions of development culminated after 1945 in Truman's version of development, according to which Europe and North America are claimed to have been entrusted by modern history with the task of developing the Global South, and Africa in particular, in its image.[20] Many contemporary ideas and practices of development can be traced to the late 1940s through to the 1950s. Development Studies as an interdisciplinary and transdisciplinary field of inquiry has been around since about the 1950s.[21] Although scholars do not provide the exact date around which the discourse of Development Studies emerged, many agree that the 1949 inaugural speech by United States President Harry S. Truman was a defining moment in the history of present development discourses. An excerpt of his speech reads as follows: 'We must embark on a bold new program for making the benefits of our scientific advances and industrial progress available for the improvement and growth of underdeveloped areas.'[22]

Without a doubt, 'development' in Truman's terms was understood as a 'Euro–American missionary task of saving and developing the Global South in general and Africa in particular'.[23] This Eurocentric narrative of development as an exogenous saving mission perpetuates the colonial idea of portraying Africans as objects of European development. Daniel Lerner affirms this problematic view, pompously claiming that 'the only hope for non-European nations is to be modernized by an injection of Western values and expertise'.[24] At the centre of Truman's version of development is what Cheru terms 'the imperial project',[25] which is informed by geopolitical considerations and the Global North's power calculations, as well as a consistent rhetoric of humanitarianism that conceals coloniality. The Truman perspective of developmentalism can be traced back to what became known as the 'voyages of discovery' in the fifteenth century, which opened the way for mercantilism, the slave trade, imperialism and colonialism. These processes were articulated, from a colonial perspective, as entailing the spread of civilization, modernity, commerce and Christianity to places

20 Ndlovu-Gatsheni, "The African Idea of Development," 4.

21 Buch-Hansen and Lauridsen, "The Past, Present and Future," 293.

22 Truman, *Point Four*, 1.

23 Thandika Mkandawire, "Running While Others Walk: Knowledge and the Challenge of Africa's Development," *Africa Development* 26, no. 2 (2011): 7–8.

24 Lerner, *The Passing of Traditional Society*, 1.

25 Cheru, "Development in Africa."

such as Africa, which was described as the 'heart of darkness' by Joseph Conrad, in his eponymous novella.[26]

Modernization theory, which is sometimes called developmentalism or the development doctrine and which emerged around the 1950s, supplied the working concepts through which Western Europe understood its 'obligation' towards those countries it considered unindustrialized, underdeveloped newly independent nations in the last half of the twentieth century.[27] According to modernization theorists, their episteme is based on claims of conscious, purposeful, nonviolent change.[28] Their pronouncements depict development as a unilateral colonial mission and thus only administered by Europeans; at the same time, they denied any African achievements before their arrival on the continent. However, as Lushaba reminds us, we should keep in mind that the year 1950 does not mark the beginning of the continent's engagement with the question of development, even if it is a watershed moment in the long tortuous sequence of 'development' along Eurocentric lines in Africa: the historiography of development in Africa, in a wider sense, both as a concept and as a process, long predates 1950.[29]

Modernization focuses on what were considered the deficiencies of countries viewed as less developed according to Eurocentric standards. Therefore, modernization prescribed how those countries labelled as underdeveloped in the Global South could overcome their deficiencies to assume an accepted standard of development, defined in terms of European standards. Development in this context simply meant an effort for the underdeveloped to catch up with the industrialized Western world. This catch-up doctrine is traceable, among other things, to Rostow's construct of growth stages.[30] The issue has recently been articulated by leading African intellectual voices such as Thandika Mkandawire as follows:

> The idea of 'catching up' entails learning not only about ideas from abroad but also about one's capacities and weaknesses. 'Catching up' requires that countries know themselves and their own history

---

26 Joseph Conrad, *Heart of Darkness and Other Stories* (London: Wordsworth Editions, 1902).

27 Nick Cullather, "Development Doctrine and Modernization Theory," *Encyclopedia of American Foreign Policy* (New York, NY: Scribner, 2002), 1.

28 Peter Stewart and Moipone Rakolojane, *Development Theories: Only Study Guide for DVA3701* (Pretoria: UNISA, 2016).

29 Lushaba, *Development as Modernity*, 1.

30 Walt W. Rostow, *The Stages of Economic Growth* (Cambridge: Cambridge University Press, 1960).

> that has set the 'initial conditions' for any future progress. They need a deep understanding of their culture, not only for self-reaffirmation, but in order to capture the strong points of their culture and institution that will see their societies through rapid social change (…).[31]

The theory of modernization has been challenged from the Global South perspective, particularly by leading Latin American dependency theorists, who argue that what looks like development is actually a process of 'development of underdevelopment or of dependent development'.[32,33] The primary argument advanced by these theorists is that the more powerful states (the Global North) take wealth from the weaker states (the Global South). They believe that weaker countries are funding the growth of the stronger countries. The very idea of development assistance from wealthy states is seen as exploitative, paternalistic and coercive, objectivizing the dependent countries.

Modernization theory has also been challenged by critical counterpoint approaches, which criticize the fact that modernization processes take the form of large-scale industrialization, urbanization and bureaucratization. These large-scale processes tend to ignore the role of local cultures; thus, they are top-down at best. Pieterse notes that the dissatisfaction in the 1970s with mainstream development has crystallized into alternative, people-centred, participatory approaches to development.[34] However, he argues that the alternative development approach has failed to offer a real alternative, as it is still trapped in the prescriptions of Western modernity.[35] The only thing that is different is that it proposes the attainment of these Western ideals through a different methodology.

It is against these ideas that this study argues that the notion and practice of development remains trapped, even today, within the European imperialist project that seeks to justify colonialism of the non-Europeans, Africans in particular, as a 'civilizing' mission aimed at bringing development to a part of the world that had remained outside of history.[36] What is perplexing about this view of development is the deliberate inability to account historically for the depravity of European colonization and the disruptions it has caused by

---

31 Mkandawire, "Running while Others Walk," 13.

32 Buch-Hansen and Laurids S. Lauridsen, "The Past, Present and Future," 293.

33 Stewart and Rakolojane, *Development Theories.*

34 Jan Nederveen Pieterse, *My Paradigm or Yours? Alternative Development, Post-Development, Reflexive Development* (Institute of Social Studies: Working Paper Series No. 229, 1996), 3.

35 Pieterse, *My Paradigm or Yours?*

36 Lushaba, *Development as Modernity*, 2.

disintegrating the cultures of those who became its victims. The colonially inspired idea of development was established through domination and taking from others, thus impoverishing them to benefit the establishment and empowerment of Europeans. In this regard, Plaatjie demonstrates that, while the mantra of the fifteenth century was to civilize and enlighten the 'soul-less' subalterns of the globe and to rescue them from their barbarity, which from a European perspective was seen as a development project, at the same time, the worst forms of barbarism were being perpetrated on the colonized, and this is the darker side of this notion of development.[37]

The groundbreaking book by Rodney, *How Europe Underdeveloped Africa*, published in 1972,[38] also exposes how European colonial regimes deliberately exploited and underdeveloped Africa. Rodney shifts the geography of analysis by clearly articulating the ripples of colonialism from Africa's viewpoint. He shows the comparative nature of the concept of development in terms of which Africa, Latin America and Asia are viewed as underdeveloped *in comparison* to Europe.[39] The unbalanced pattern of development is created by the fact that Europe as the 'exploiter' becomes developed, while the 'exploited' becomes underdeveloped. The very vocabulary of describing some as developed and others as underdeveloped implies a discriminatory and racist worldview premised on European hegemonic standards.

It is therefore the contention of this study that modernization theory has nothing to do with development, conceived as philanthropic handouts towards non-Europeans. Instead, this theory peddles coloniality-anchored perspectives to conceptualize development. The most culpable aspect of this perspective's hypocrisy is its concealment of the effects of Europe's underdevelopment on Africa. The modernization theory is also a smokescreen for European racism against non-Europeans, who are misrepresented as beneficiaries of European development's benevolence. In essence, the modernization theory represents a Eurocentric fundamental order and its exclusionist insinuations, suggesting that Europe is the epitome of modernization and a barometer of the apex of civilization.

Europe has effectively granted itself the right violently to impose its autonomy on those it categorizes as underdeveloped in a bid to 'redeem' them from their

37 Sebeka Richard Plaatjie, "Beyond Western-centric and Eurocentric Development: A Case for Decolonizing Development," *Africanus Journal of Development Studies* 43, no. 2 (2013): 124.

38 Rodney, *How Europe Underdeveloped Africa.*

39 Rodney, *How Europe Underdeveloped Africa.*

primitivism and traditionalism. It is in this context that Césaire's *Discourse on Colonialism* speaks of Western civilization as colonialism.[40] In fact, Césaire's question about what colonialism is fundamentally unmasks the rhetoric of 'development' as a cover-up for deeper forms of colonialism. These forms of colonialism go into the psyche of the colonized subjects while affecting and re-articulating their power, knowledge, being and nature. The idea of development as an imitative process for Europe and North America's non-European counterparts to follow therefore conceals the unfairness of the premise on which that process is based. It raises fundamental questions about the Western development project: *Should* Africa catch up with a process founded on colonialism and imperialism and the objectivization of others? *Should* colonialism and the suppression of others be deemed a morally acceptable method of attaining so-called progress?

It is crucial to reflect on the implications of European notions of development because they have contributed to environmental decay in the pursuit of economic wealth creation for European nations. When the idea of development harms the very environment we depend on for our survival, surely it is founded on undesirable values. Escobar demonstrates in frightening detail how the theory and practice of development are characterized by serious errors in terms of cultural bias, misunderstanding and failed promises.[41] He argues that there is no linear model of economic and social development that can be accurately applied to the diverse local cultures of all those societies misleadingly grouped under the 'Third World' label.[42] The very construction of the term 'Third World is an

> [...] ethnocentric invention of the post-World War II era; and development is an equally flawed 'regime of representation' crafted from a conflicting ensemble of ideology, partial interests and the attempts of the West (especially the United States) to impose its power-driven interests on non-Western peoples.[43]

Esteva and Prakash add their voices to these debates by arguing that

> almost two billion people became under-developed overnight in the post-war era, with the launching of global development, they were placed

40 Aimé Césaire, *Discourse on Colonialism* (New York, NY: Monthly Review Press, 1955), 2.
41 Escobar, *Encountering Development*, 1–17.
42 Escobar, *Encountering Development*, 9.
43 Escobar, *Encountering Development*, 10–11.

> in undignified position of having started on the road that others know better towards a goal that others have reached, a one-way street.[44]

This way of thinking about development contributed to the marginalization of non-Europeans, and Africans in particular, and presented them as objects waiting to be developed by Western Europe which assumed a superior position and belittled the rest. Mehmet is another author who notes that 'Europeans became the agents of development while Africans became the objects of development'.[45]

Hence, the current study calls for the decolonization of the very idea of development conceptualized as the civilizing mission that objectifies Africans. The study advances the view that development should be informed by the historical journey, cultural dynamics and knowledge of those at the centre of the development process. It should not be a hegemonic process, but rather a liberating one, and it must be endogenous. Thus, from the perspective of the Global South and Africa in particular, the discourse of development needs to be redeemed from hegemonic Eurocentric views and must be relocated within the epistemologies of the Global South, including Africa.

Africa's Journey with Development under Post-colonial Administrations

Africa's struggle to develop should be understood within the historical context of the factors that have shaped the continent – in particular, the colonial legacy. For this reason, African conceptions of development in the post-independence era continue to be informed by the Truman version of developmentalism. The African nation-building projects in the post-colonial era still adopt modernist-elitist models informed by Western ideals. According to Baah, the very construction and stratification of the present continent of Africa into 54 nation-states was not mapped by Africans, but by imperialists whose selfish ambitions did not include the socio-economic development interests of the continent.[46]

Ndlovu-Gatsheni posits that

> when the Organization of African Unity (OAU) at its formation in 1963 accepted the principle of the inviolability of the existing boundaries

44 Esteva and Prakash, "Beyond Development, What?," 282.

45 Ozay Mehmet, *Westernizing the Third World: The Eurocentricity of Economic Development Theories* (London and New York, NY: Routledge, 1995), 9.

46 Baah, *History of African Development Initiatives*, 1.

> inherited from the colonial era and the Berlin consensus of 1884–1885, it became clear that the decolonization struggle was permeated by what Frantz Fanon [...] labelled repetition without change.[47,48]

The implication is clear: African leaders themselves failed to reconstruct and re-stratify the continent after their own imagination and, as a result, the borders imposed by the Berlin Conference became legitimized as a point of departure for the Organization of African Unity. The failure of African leaders to change the stratification of the continent must be understood in the context of neocolonialism, which continued its assault on Africa.

Prior to colonialism, African people, like all other human beings, constantly and consistently improved the quality of their lives; however, the negative impact of the 1884–1885 Berlin Scramble for Africa left a permanent mark on Africa's territories from which its people are still seeking to extricate themselves. The post-independence era meant that the new African leaders faced the mammoth task of rebuilding ravaged economies to improve the quality of life of all Africans. Moreover, according to Alemazung, 'when colonialism finally ended the Western powers could not afford to keep their hands completely off these regions, thus they continued to indirectly influence local politics and development trajectory'.[49] Talton also notes that 'culturally and politically, the legacy of European dominance remained evident in the national borders, political infrastructure, education systems, national languages, economics, and trade networks of each former colony'.[50] This legacy means that Africa, even after independence, continues to be shaped by the imprint of its former colonial masters.

Nkrumah in *Neo-colonialism: The Last Stage of Imperialism* also describes a situation where former colonial empires continue to exercise control over their erstwhile colonies through indirect methods such as the use of trade relations as a mechanism to thwart growth.[51] Neocolonialism has come to be seen more generally as involving a coordinated effort by the former

---

47 Ndlovu-Gatsheni, "The Entrapment of Africa," 345.

48 Frantz Fanon, *The Wretched of the Earth* (New York, NY: Grove Press, 1968), 23–25, cited in Ndlovu-Gatsheni, 345.

49 Joy Asongazoh Alemazung, "Post-Colonial Colonialism: An Analysis of International Factors and Actors Marring African Socio-Economic and Political Development," *Journal of Pan African Studies* 3, no. 10 (2010): 64.

50 Benjamin Talton, *The Challenge of Decolonization in Africa* (2017) [Online], 1.

51 Nkrumah, *Neo-Colonialism.*

colonial powers and other developed countries to block growth in developing countries and retain them as sources of cheap raw materials and labour. This is why Ndlovu-Gatsheni posits that

> [a]fter political independence beginning with Ghana in 1957, African leaders pursued nation-building and development as critical interconnected goals in an effort to 'remembering' the dismembered African societies and peoples so as to regain their dislocated ontological density and attain unity.[52]

Most African leaders adopted human-centred development strategies after independence with the main objective of freeing Africans from the inimical legacies of enslavement, colonialism, imperialism, apartheid and underdevelopment, as well as the imposed Washington Consensus and neocolonialism. African alternative conceptions of human development should be understood as a struggle for what Ngugi wa Thiong'o[53] understands as a re-membering – the quest for wholeness for people who have been marginalized and dismembered for a period of 500 years of European modernity. Humanism in African thought is then seen as the central theme of nation-building and development for people whose very being has been questioned and denied. In the words of former Zambian President Kenneth Kaunda, 'humanism is defined as the "philosophy of life" to correct the devaluing of humanity emanating from colonialism'.[54] African humanism was conceived as an alternative decolonial version of development vision, and it challenges the hegemonic Eurocentric idea of development rooted in the modernization paradigm.

It is in this context that an African humanist orientation to development should be understood as an alternative African development path, as there was a strong feeling that imperialism, colonialism and apartheid were processes that resulted in the marginalization and dehumanization of Africans. The leitmotif of humanism has resulted in experimentation with African socialism, with 'Ujamaa' (Family-hood) in Tanzania under

---

52 Ndlovu-Gatsheni, "The African Idea of Development," 6.

53 Ngugi wa Thiong'o, *Something Torn and New: An African Renaissance* (New York, NY: Basic Civitas Books, 2009); Ngugi wa Thiong'o, *Re-membering Africa* (Nairobi: East African Publishers, 2009).

54 Kaunda, Kenneth D. and Colin M. Morris, *A Humanist in Africa: Letters to Colin M. Morris from Kenneth D. Kaunda, President of Zambia* (Nashville, TN and New York, NY: Abingdon Press, 1966), 20.

its first post-independence president, Julius Nyerere, as the most notable example:

> Nyerere's philosophy of *Ujamaa* was rooted in traditional African values and had as its core the emphasis on family-hood and communalism of traditional African societies. Ujamaa was founded on a philosophy of development that was based on three essentials – freedom, equality and unity.[55]

Nyerere was not alone in this path, as already noted, as most African nationalists co-partnered in this vision: 'Kwame Nkrumah's agenda for "social revolution", Leopold Senghor's "negritude" and Kenneth Kaunda's "Zambian Humanism"'[56] – all displayed a similar attitude in orientation to counter the legacies of African marginalization and underdevelopment by European powers. Ndlovu-Gatsheni[57] further highlights that the search for a humane society by African nationalists was further exemplified by charters and declarations such as the *Freedom Charter* (South Africa), the *Arusha Declaration* (Tanzania), the *Common Man's Charter* (Uganda) and the *Mulugushi Declaration* (Zambia). These charters and declarations were grounded on the African nationalist humanist imaginations of a better world, free from domination, racism and exploitation.

However, these initiatives were not easy to implement, as a result of interference by the Western powers. Hence, from the start of the 1970s, the growth profile of most African countries began to decline sharply, and it became clear by the mid-1980s that these economies would need financial rescue packages in the form of financial relief. Numerous factors were cited for this sharp decline, among them overinvestment in the social sector; for example, 'in Ghana, 62 per cent of all investment was directed to social services'.[58] This was seen as the consequence of the human-centred approach to development, which was deemed less competitive than the free market economic development path. According to Alemazung, neocolonial relations created African leaders who became European patrons – a result was that leaders participated in corrupt practices as they sought to protect their own interests at the expense of the people they led.[59] A high level of

55 Bonny Ibhawoh and J. I. Dibua, "Deconstructing *Ujamaa*: The Legacy of Julius Nyerere in the Quest for Social and Economic Development in Africa," *African Journal of Political Science* 8 (2003): 62.

56 Ibhawoh and Dibua, "Deconstructing *Ujamaa*," 62.

57 Ndlovu-Gatsheni, "The African Idea of Development," 8.

58 Baah, *History of African Development Initiatives*, 2.

59 Alemazung, "Post-Colonial Colonialism," 69.

corruption among officials was soon cited as the main reason for economic decline in the aftermath of political independence. Perron (1989) also notes that the international oil shock of 1973 had a further negative effect on the global economy and imposed heavy debt on African countries. Alemazung,[60] Baah[61] and Talton[62] cite the lasting effects of the Cold War as another key contributing factor to the economic decline in African countries.

The Western powers viewed African states at independence through the lens of the Cold War, which categorized African leaders as either pro-West (leaning towards free market ideologies) or pro-East (leaning towards pro-socialist ideologies). As part of the strategy to escape ideological rivalry between the East and West, African countries joined forces with the Asian countries in 1955 in what became known as the Bandung Conference, whose main aim was to hasten the process of decolonization through Afro-Asiatic solidarity and to create conditions for global peaceful coexistence in the post–World War II landscape, which continued to be characterized by ideological competition between the West and the East. The tensions of Cold War politics deprived these initiatives of the ability to empower Africa to shape its own autonomous development path, which was inward-looking.

Adedeji also argues that the development merchant system driven by the Bretton Woods Institutions,[63] namely the World Bank and International Monetary Fund (IMF), effectively destabilized African initiatives and ensured that African states cannot operate independently from Euro-North American development orthodoxy and coloniality.[64] The Western powers saw alternative humanist development strategies by African leaders as a threat to the free market ideology. They therefore sought to interfere in Africa's political and economic affairs through these international financial institutions (the World Bank and IMF). These powers kept Africa's development journey trapped in coloniality.

According to Baah, as part of strategies to restore their declining economies, African leaders proposed regional integration as a strategy to foster cooperation[65]; the Economic Community of West African States (ECOWAS) and the East African Community (EAC) were established: 'In 1979, the EAC

60 Alemazung, "Post-Colonial Colonialism."

61 Baah, *History of African Development Initiatives.*

62 Talton, *The Challenge of Decolonization.*

63 Adebayo Adedeji, *From the Lagos Plan of Action to the New Partnership for African Development and from the Final Act of Lagos to the Constitutive Act: Whither Africa?* (Keynote address at African Forum for Envisioning Africa, Nairobi, Kenya, 29 April 2002), 4.

64 Ndlovu-Gatsheni, "The African Idea of Development," 12.

65 Baah, *History of African Development Initiatives*, 4.

[East African Community] drafted a document entitled "*Revised framework for principles of the new international order in Africa*", which was followed by the Lagos Plan of Action (LPA) in the 1980s'.[66] The Lagos Plan of Action identified Africa's development woes as structural and as exacerbated by a hostile external environment. Despite the fact that the Lagos Plan of Action was criticized as a top-down project that focused mainly on external influence on Africa but did not focus on the internal problems of African leaders themselves, it was another effort by African leaders to find a way out of their development challenges. According to Ikome, the Lagos Plan of Action 'itself did not represent complete de-linking of African from the West but sought to strategically disengage from those features of international economic systems that was keeping Africa dependent, underdeveloped and marginalized'.[67]

These African initiatives advocated a development strategy with self-reliance, democratization and the just distribution of wealth as its core principles. Unfortunately, these initiatives failed to improve the situation. One of the main reasons was that the international financial institutions imposed their own recommendations in the form of structural adjustment programmes. Implemented from the beginning of the 1980s through to the 1990s, the policies of these programmes focused on privatization, liberalization and fiscal austerity, which directly contradicted African leaders' initiatives. Stiglitz (2002) argues that many of these structural adjustment programmes and policies became an end in themselves rather than a means to equitable and sustainable growth.[68] Therien warns that it is vital to comprehend those international financial institutions[69]: through the structural adjustment programmes and neoliberal policies (sometimes collectively called the Washington Consensus), they 'were pursuing the Bretton Woods paradigm of development which is entrapped within the exogenous development mission'.[70]

While the highlighted factors are cited as the real causes behind Africa's apparently dismal 'failure to develop', it remains important to interpret them within the context of a history of five centuries of imperialism, colonialism, enslavement and the dehumanization of the African people. The very framework against which the notion of progress in Africa was (and is) measured

66 Baah, *History of African Development Initiatives*, 4.

67 Francis Nguendi Ikome, *From LPA to NEPAD: The Political Economy of African Regional Initiatives* (Midrand: Institute for Global Dialogue, 2007), 7.

68 Joseph E. Stiglitz, *Globalization and Its Discontents* (New York, NY: Norton, 2002).

69 Jean-Philippe Therien, "Beyond the North-South Divide: The Two Tales of World Poverty," *Third World Quarterly* 20, no. 4 (1999): 723–42.

70 Therien, "Beyond the North-South Divide."

was itself predetermined by Eurocentric standards of modernity. These are not informed by an African-defined view of progress but by an imposed Eurocentric view, which continues to portray the continent as a hegemonized space, physically and ideologically. As part of the strategy to overcome this legacy, the spirit of the Bandung Conference (1955) must be resuscitated to enable the liberation of the development discourse in Africa and to give power to African leaders and the masses to speak in their own voices, for their own liberation. History has proven that the role of Bretton Woods Institutions in Africa has been to sustain the interventionist Eurocentric idea of Truman's development mission. Hence, it is the view of this study that the genealogy of development intervention from the West since independence has continued the historical objectification of Africans and sustained Euro-American hegemony over Africa.

Mapping the Future of an African Development Trajectory beyond Eurocentrism

Afrocentricity as a guiding theoretical framework proposes that we must transcend the narrow Eurocentric framework in our interpretation of the idea and practice of development in Africa. Asante argues that we cannot understand Africa's contribution to its own development and the world without examining the basis for society.[71] Therefore, Afrocentricity's call is about the need to relocate African people within their own history and culture as a necessary base from which to conceptualize their development future.

Asante offers Afrocentricity as an ethical intellectual standpoint that seeks to empower Africans to become the subjects of their own development.[72] The understanding and interpretation of development should therefore be framed within the historical and cultural narratives of African people as centred to properly serve their own interests. African resurgence will never take place until Africans champion a renaissance grounded in a new paradigm of dramatic narratives of victory.[73]

Afrocentricity is premised on the argument that all knowledge results from an occasion of encounter in a particular place. Thus, without being centred in a place, Africans will continue to imbibe other people's narratives as though they are theirs. Until such time that Africans claim the classical past of their ancestors in Kemet (Egypt), the story of African development

71 Asante, *An Afrocentric Manifesto: Toward an African Renaissance*, 66.

72 Asante, *The Afrocentric Idea* (rev., exp. ed.), xii.

73 Asante, *African Pyramids of Knowledge*, 1.

will remain incorrectly narrated, and we will continue to hold on to mere half-truths. Asante supports his proposition by arguing that 'the ancient people of ancient Egypt who lived along the banks of the Nile River took advantage of whatever situation was presented to them by the river's flow'.[74] He demonstrates this point as follows:

> If the river was full of water, the Kemites (ancient Egyptians) used large barges to float stones to various sites. If the river had little water, they used heavy sledges pulled by hundreds of people over constantly replaced wooden rollers. Every day was one of decision-making in the best interest of society.[75]

It would thus be incorrect to suggest that Africans did not develop on their own and were merely unknowable subjects who waited to be developed by European interventions that started in the 1950s after World War II, as suggested by Harry S. Truman's Point Four program.[76] Unless Africans reclaim their history, they cannot define any future. Rather, they will continue to be replicas of the histories of other nations and be permanently dependent people. The challenge facing African scholars is to debunk the Western narrative rooted in the Greek philosophical foundation that presents the West as the sole originator of civilization. Stepping outside of the historical moments as narrated by European scholars would permit new interpretations and the acquisition of new knowledge about Africa.

Lushaba also affirms that 'it is time for Africa to reclaim its autonomy of thought and seek to understand our own reality without the authority of others'.[77] The restoration of the dismembered ontological density of Africans created throughout Western historiography and the Berlin Scramble meant that for true development to occur in Africa, Western epistemologies must be questioned, analysed and rejected in favour of African-centred narratives. In this context, it is important to remind ourselves that Ngugi wa Thiong'o frames African conceptions of development as a struggle for re-membering Africa after the Berlin Scramble.[78] Re-membering can be understood as the African quest for wholeness after more than five centuries of dis-memberment.

---

74 Asante, *African Pyramids of Knowledge*, 1.

75 Asante, *African Pyramids of Knowledge*, 2.

76 Truman, *Point Four.*

77 Lushaba, *Development as Modernity*, 58.

78 Ngugi wa Thiong'o, *Re-membering Africa.*

Afrocentricity, therefore, challenges all faculties of social sciences and policymakers to shift the geography of reason and analysis from Euro-centredness to Africa-centredness. This means that the idea and practice of development should be engaged from a position of Africans as centred and rooted in their own existential realities. Africans should engage with development not as dependent beneficiaries of European-conceived ideas of development, but as people capable of defining their own needs and solving their own challenges.

This means that the idea of development should not be interpreted solely to mean economic freedom and overcoming the scourge of poverty in Africa, as this would be a narrow interpretation. Modernization as a perspective has used wealth (and economic indicators) as a primary indicator to determine the level of a country's progress (Regan, 2006:22). This way of measuring development fails to account for the social, political and cultural aspects of development. This approach is now giving way to the Human Development Index (HDI), which was devised by the United Nations Development Programme and is now employed as a measure of development or human progress and quality of life by many countries. This indicator, among other things, looks at life expectancy, education and income in the individual country (Regan, 2006). There is also an emerging pan-African-centred perspective focusing on the 'human-factor' approach to development.[79] This view holds that human capital is a valuable asset in promoting development. Therefore, development practitioners and participants must have a self-driven attitude and positive orientation towards a particular angle of development that they expect in critical areas of their respective countries' needs. This implies that the pace of any development prospect must be determined by localized expectations of the worldview of the countries concerned.

It is then the mandate of the human factor (practitioners' and participants') approach to correlate the expected function with societal growth in critical gaps to promote sustainable human livelihoods. The human factor approach and its Afrocentric underpinnings are more relevant to Africa than the modernization model. This is confirmed by the continent's need to develop beyond economic limitations, which the modernization perspective on development has inscribed and reinforced. The limited relevance of the modernization theory is exposed by the realities of the multiple destructive effects of colonialism and slavery. These effects were not only

79 Vimbai G. Chivaura and Claude G. Mararike, *The Human Factor Approach to Development in Africa* (Harare: University of Zimbabwe Publications, 1998).

economically and politically catastrophic to Africa's growth but led directly to the stagnation of the gradual growth of sustainable sources of human livelihood on the continent. The enormity of the realities that the task of development must face in Africa calls for an epistemic transition from the Eurocentric modernization articulation of development towards an Afrocentric paradigm.

This perspective is informed by the merits of Afrocentricity's inclusive character in unpacking the African development agenda beyond narrow Eurocentric/economic-centred aspects of development, as espoused in the modernization theory, which neglects the human factor question. The modernization school of thought has sought to account for the level of development of those considered 'developing nations' by using the wrong indicators altogether. For this reason, this study argues that using Eurocentric standards is misleading and merely builds on stereotypes of what progress and development are supposed to be in multicultural societies in Africa. As far back as 1980, Asante already noted that the Eurocentric view had become an ethnocentric view that elevated the European experience and downgraded all others and that foregrounding and exposing this epistemological abuse is essential if Africa is to displace Eurocentrism in all its many aspects from African lives, be it economic, social, political, cultural or religious.[80]

The Afrocentric development paradigm should therefore enable a relocation of Africans to their own cultural context. From that context, they are able to become their own agents and subjects. That said, this study proposes that development, as Chukwuokolo also suggests,[81] be understood to involve a holistic evaluative process of the epistemic, cultural, economic, political, religious, normative, psychological and sociological stance of African people. Chukwuokolo's view affirms the expressions of the Bandung Conference of 1955, which perceived development as a redemptive human aspiration: development should promote the attainment of freedom from the political, economic, ideological, epistemological and social domination instilled through colonialism and coloniality.[82] This conception of development offers a more holistic picture and seeks to resist reductionist tendencies to measure development as solely an economic project, disregarding other contributing aspects.

The conception of an Afrocentric development paradigm should be framed from a clear understanding of African classical history in a pre-colonial era,

80 Asante, *Afrocentricity: The Theory of Social Change.*

81 Chukwuokolo, "Afrocentrism or Eurocentrism."

82 Ndlovu-Gatsheni, *Coloniality of Power.*

the impact of a colonial expedition and the aftermath of the post-colonial era. A historical understanding of how the African continent advanced itself prior to colonization would enable a proper account of the factors that have limited African people from realizing their dreams of a better quality of life. This is to counter the effects of the fact that, as Mazrui points out, what Africa knows about itself, what different parts of Africa know about each other, has been profoundly influenced by the West.[83]

Ndlovu-Gatsheni[84] highlights six long-term effects of colonialism in Africa as identified by Mazrui.[85] First, colonialism and capitalism forcibly incorporated Africa into the world economy, beginning with the slave trade. Second, the exclusion of Africa from the post-1648 Westphalian sovereign state system and the physical scramble for Africa after the 1884–1885 Berlin Conference, and the incorporation of Africa into the post-1945 United Nations state system has shaped Africa's position in the global sphere to this day. Third, the incorporation of Africa into the Euro-North American-centric world culture and European languages has had a deep impact. Fourth, the incorporation of Africa into a heavily Euro-North American-centric world of international law has reshaped its trajectory. Fifth, Africa has been incorporated into the modern technological age, including being enmeshed in the global system of dissemination of information. Last, Africa has been swallowed up into a Euro-North American-centred moral order that claims to be dominated by Christian thought.

The unmasking of the above hegemonic factors would enable a logical explanation of why Africa as a continent is less developed in comparison to Europe and North America. The historically based account would dispel the myths imposed by European scholars such as Hegel, who propounded that 'Africa only hears the echo of the majestic march of world civilization across Europe and through which the absolute spirit fulfils and realizes itself'.[86] Such revelations would deconstruct the negative images that have been implanted to depict Africans as zoo-bound people who lack philosophy, which is humankind's greatest intellectual achievement.

Moreover, an honest historical analysis of the continent's contribution to world civilization would end the tendency to teach half-truths, which Eurocentrists have deliberately used as a strategy to suppress Africans so that they cannot know themselves and thus to ensure that they will never rise to oppose

83 Ali A. Mazrui, *The Africans: A Triple Heritage* (London: BBC Publication, 1986).

84 Ndlovu-Gatsheni, Sabelo J., "Decoloniality as the Future of Africa," 485–96.

85 Mazrui, *The Africans: A Triple Heritage.*

86 Hegel, quoted in Chukwuokolo, "Afrocentrism or Eurocentrism," 29.

their oppressors. In the same way, European colonization has dismembered Africa to be a replica of Europe and planted its memories in the psyche of Africans to reproduce itself. An Afrocentric development paradigm must undertake the re-membering of Africa and improve Africans' quality of life. An Afrocentric development idea should end the alienation of Africans and reorient them to themselves, as well as prioritize their cultural expressions. It is within this context that Ngugi Wa Thiong'o in *Moving the Centre: The Struggle for Cultural Freedoms*[87] argues that the centre should be moved from its assumed location in the West to a multiplicity of spheres in all the cultures of the world, Africa in particular as the centre of analysis for Africans. What this means for the study of development is that African-centred perspectives must inform how Africans conceptualize their own development, thus overcoming the hegemony of Euro-centredness.

The narration of the discourse of development from an Afrocentric perspective will enable Africans to overcome what Chambers refers to as the 'outsider perspective'.[88] Mafeje, an African scholar and a social anthropologist, argues that social science disciplines (including Development Studies) still suffer from an 'epistemology of alterity', which refers to a scholarship rooted in Western thought.[89] Mafeje emphasizes the 'insistence on Africans to think, speak, and do things for themselves in the first place. This does not imply an unwillingness to learn from others, but this is a rebellion to domination by others, irrespective of colour or race'.[90] In essence, the Afrocentric development paradigm is about Africans defining development for themselves and determining what best suits African circumstances, thus overcoming European paternalism.

---

87 Ngugi wa Thiong'o, *Moving the Centre: The Struggle for Cultural Freedoms* (London: James Currey, 1993).

88 Chambers, *Rural Development*, 2–3.

89 Dastile, "Beyond Euro-Western Dominance," 97.

90 Quoted in Dastile, "Beyond Euro-Western Dominance," 97.

Chapter 4

AFROCENTRICITY ON THE SIGNIFICANCE OF AFRICAN HISTORY FOR DEVELOPMENT

Marcus Garvey, a noted Pan-Africanist activist, journalist and entrepreneur, wrote that 'a people without knowledge of their historical past and culture is like a tree without roots. When all we know is the history written by those who conquered us, we remain shackled and submerged beneath their own narratives.'[1]

The story of Africa's development trajectory must be anchored within our own African narratives. Throughout its unfolding as a theory of social change, Afrocentricity has consistently and systematically rewritten African history as a contribution to African development itself, and as part of the broader agenda of the restoration of African humanity. The objective of an Afrocentric historicism is to rediscover Africa's contributions to human civilization as the launching pad for Africa's rediscovery of itself, as opposed to the current habit of Africans always seeking to adjust to the European game plan. Thus, in Afrocentricity, an understanding of the corrected record of Africa's historical trajectory is a prerequisite for Africa's reconceptualization of its own development ideal. At the centre of an African reawakening must lie the imperative of understanding how the people of this continent have lived in their own environment to improve their quality of life. This implies that consistently and systematically challenging Eurocentric negative tropes about Africa as an uncivilized, unmodern, underdeveloped and backward continent is part of Afrocentricity's work of reclaiming their history from Eurocentric distortions and of countering the falsification of information about Africa.[2]

The theft of Africa's history has gone hand in hand with a denial of African genius and agency. The consistent pattern of the negation of

1 Cherron Inko-Tariah MBE, B: M2022, 1.

2 Asante, *Facing South to Africa.*

Africa by European writers has contributed to a denigration of African voices and to a devaluing of African contributions to world civilization. It is against this pervasive European epistemic injustice against Africans that Afrocentricity as a paradigm of the African Renaissance is committed to addressing the need for history to be reinterpreted from a perspective in which African people stand as subjects and not objects of European analysis. Moreover, Afrocentric historiography provides a clearer perspective on Africa's pursuit for Africa's own advancement. Thus, the discourse of development in Africa must be liberated from the factors that have negatively shaped Africa and its people, relegating them to the lower political, social and economic structures of the modern world system, which continues to be dominated by Europe and North America. Hence, the interrogation of the role of African history in Africa's own development enables a fuller perspective that could enable Africa's resurgence to its former greatness and glory. To attain this desirable ideal, it will require Africans to deepen their commitment to decolonization – political, economic and epistemological – to end the dislocation created through coloniality.

We must interrogate Eurocentric historiography and its negative views regarding Africa's contribution to human civilization as a way to rebel against domination. The call, therefore, is to be immersed in the re-narration of an Afrocentric historiography, grounded on the theory of Afrocentricity, to debunk the negation of Africa by European scholars. Detailed reflections on the work of African scholars such as Cheikh Anta Diop, George G. M. James, Theophile Obenga, Maulana Karenga, Ama Mazama, Molefi Kete Asante and Kwame Nkrumah and the works of many other various Afrocentric scholars must inform a legitimate understanding of the subject of Africa's own development in order to attain African re-humanization and overcome the development impasse in the post-colonial epoch.

Eurocentric Historiography and the Negation of Africa's Contribution to World Civilization

According to Asante,[3] what makes Africa a complex area of study is that Europe continues to present itself as the source of information about Africa, to the neglect of African imaginations of themselves. Similarly, Gordon argues that 'throughout the 19th and most of the 20th century, African history and African historiography were dominated by Western grand narratives of how

3 Asante, *An Afrocentric Manifesto: Toward an African Renaissance*, 55.

Europeans interpreted the world'.[4] In discussing Africa, European historians distorted the image of Africans, resulting in a form of history that those engaged in colonizing Africa used as propaganda to expand Europe through the invasion of Africa, while presenting Africa and Africans in a negative light. Thus, the inferiorization of Africa became part of the philosophical and cultural fabric of Europeanization. Adeleke concludes that the African experience worldwide, since the rise of modern Europe, has endured the burden of Western history, which is the history of negation.[5] 'Enlightened' Europeans used racist epithets such as 'the dark continent', 'heathens', 'savages' and 'barbarians' as a way to negate Africans as human beings capable of producing any civilization. These pejorative views nullified African history, culture and agency and mandated Europeans to lead Africans towards civilization.[6,7]

The fifteenth-century European 'voyages of discovery' which opened the way for mercantilism, the slave trade, imperialism and colonialism were motivated from a colonial perspective by the mission to spread civilization, modernity and Christianity to places such as Africa, which were described as the 'heart of darkness'.[8] The grand theory of modernization was introduced after World War II (from 1945 onwards) as a project aimed at the civilization of Africa and was rooted in the same false narrative of European supremacy, by seeking to transplant European experiences to Africa in the hope of 'saving' Africans from what North America in particular considered to be backwardness. This view was projected from a dislocated perspective regarding Africa as a barbaric area without any history or civilization.

Prior to European colonization, African people, like all other human beings, constantly and consistently improved their lives and life chances. They were inventive and innovative in many ways. In their book *'African Intellectual Heritage': A Book of Sources*, Asante and Abarry capture African works of imagination, invention, cultural dynamism, political engineering, religious and economic sophistication and originality.[9] They demonstrate that Africans have always been active and independent domesticators of

---

4 Jacob Gordon, "Towards an African Historiography," in *Egypt vs. Greece and the American Academy: The Debate over the Birth of Civilization*, ed. Molefi Kete Asante and Ama Mazama (Chicago, IL: African American Images, 2002), 33.

5 Adeleke, "Africa and Afrocentric Historicism," 200.

6 J. M. Blaut, *The Colonizer's Model of the World: Geographical Diffusion and Eurocentric History* (New York, NY: Guilford Press, 1993).

7 Audrey Smedley, *Race in North America: The Origins and Evolution of a Worldview* (Boulder, CO: Westview, 1993).

8 Conrad, *Heart of Darkness.*

9 Asante, Molefi Kete and Abu Shardow Abarry, *African Intellectual Heritage: A Book of Sources* (Philadelphia, PA: Temple University Press, 1996).

plants and animals. They improved their technologies from stone to iron tools. They migrated from place to place in search of better environments that enhanced their life chances. They established sociopolitical systems, lineages, clans, chiefdoms, kingdoms, states and nations of varying sizes and complexities. Like all other human beings, Africans developed complex ideas as they made sense of their lives and environment.

Despite Africa's long history, European accounts of Africa continued for a long time to be the mainstream historical literature on Africa, and this situation fed the agenda of negation. Europe mobilized historians, ethnographers and philosophers by sponsoring the contemptible task of distorting historical facts about Africa.[10] According to Gordon,[11] interesting examples of such studies include Richard Burton's *Travels in Arabia and Africa* (1866) and A. P. Newton's lectures to the Royal African Society in London on 'Africa and Historical Research' (1923), in which Newton claimed that 'Africa had no history before the coming of the Europeans'.[12]

Fage also attests that many professional colonial historians who wrote more recent histories of Africa remained wedded to the concept that African people had no history, or no history that they could study or that was worth their studying.[13] Thus, for the most part, African history was written in Arabic and European languages, indicating the dominance of those cultures over African political, social and religious life.[14] The general view of European philosophers and historians, beginning in the fifteenth century, was that the only history that was of any significance was the study of 'Western civilization', from its alleged origin in ancient Greece, Rome and Judea.[15] This implies, therefore, that European historians reinvented the idea of Africa in ways that suited politicians' and economic interests' colonial mission of conquest. According to Gordon,

> [...] these historians disregarded the African origin of human civilization; indeed, they tried to disregard the African origin of the human race. Civilizations of the Nile Valley, such as the Badari, Kemetic, and Meroitic were simply dismissed as non-African although they were in Africa or ignored altogether.[16]

---

10 Chukwuokolo, "Afrocentrism or Eurocentrism," 29.

11 Gordon, "Towards an African Historiography."

12 Quoted in Gordon, "Towards an African Historiography," 26.

13 John D. Fage, *A History of West Africa: An Introductory Survey* (London: Oxford University Press, 1969).

14 Gordon, "Towards an African Historiography," 25.

15 Fage, *A History of West Africa.*

16 Fage, *A History of West Africa.*

Asante argues that European scholars sought to attack the very Africanity of the ancient Egyptians as a ploy to distort information, thus advancing their commercial greed over the symbols, icons and values of the African people.[17] Because of their colonial ambitions, Europeans took from their historians only that which was deemed to serve the European conquest agenda over Africa. Theirs was a mission to (dis)place Africa within a historical context understandable to Europeans and honouring only their own ancestors' contributions to world history.

Today, we can see and rightly critique the nefarious role played by Hegel, in particular, in this process of projecting Africa in negative terms in the social sciences. As Asante[18] explains, in Hegel's 1828 lectures on history, he supported the negative view held by his fellow European historians that Africa's role in world history should be forgotten, because it had no history nor culture to show other than barbarism. Hegel, who never even set foot in Africa, thus attacked the very humanity of African people and their world views, as a people not capable of projecting their own realities. A flood of academic writings 'proving' the inferiority of Africans accelerated the derogation of Africa.[19] Another such European historian was Hugh Trevor-Roper, the Regius Chair of Modern History at Oxford University, who, as recently as 1967, is reputed to have made the outrageous remark that what happened in Africa was no more than 'the unrewarding gyrations of barbarous tribes'.[20] Chukwuokolo[21] points out that Max Weber, a German sociologist and philosopher, was also caught up in this anti-African web when he averred that all indices for civilization existed only in Europe, namely art, music, architecture, science and other aspects of human endeavour. Weber proclaimed that

> [...] it is only in Europe that science had reached its apogee of evolution, which we recognize today as valid. Empirical knowledge, reflections on problems of the cosmos and of life, philosophical and theological wisdom of the most profound, the full development of a systematic theology must be credited to Christianity under the influence of Hellenism.[22]

---

17 Asante, *An Afrocentric Manifesto: Toward an African Renaissance*, 68.

18 Asante, *Facing South to Africa*, 115.

19 Asante, *Facing South to Africa*.

20 Hugh Trevor-Roper, Hugh, *The Rise of Christian Europe*. London: Jarrold and Sons, 1967, quoted in Gordon, "Towards an African Historiography," 34.

21 Chukwuokolo, "Afrocentrism or Eurocentrism," 30.

22 Max Weber, *The Protestant Ethic and the Spirit of Capitalism* (New York, NY: Charles Scribner's Sons, 1958), 13.

Such anti-African views were conducive to Europeans' manipulation of the consciousness of Africans to view the world from a European perspective in all spheres – social, political, developmental, religious and economic.[23] Such views have also informed many African intellectuals who received a Western education, and who therefore continue to reject Africa's contribution to world civilization and are apologists of Western political propaganda. As Asante reminds us, the colonialists did not respect or honour African terms[24]; for this reason, Africans have been moved completely away from their own terms, be they political, economic, social, linguistic or cultural. Thus, the colonization of Africa was not only a physical act but also an intellectual one:

> [...] the one objective of European colonialists was to produce in the African person an individual who was European in thought, education, behavior, attitude, opinions, and taste, artistic and otherwise, while remaining black and African only in colour. The consequences of such dislocation were enormous. It meant that Africans who had been taught in French schools 'the Gauls were their ancestors,' or the Africans in the United States of America or in the British colonies in the African continent who had been told that English literature represented the highest form of art in human history.[25]

Such pronouncements about ancestry or cultural production had the effect of moving Africans further away from their own agency, history and cultural perspectives and being infused by the colonially constructed view of reality.

Academic imperialists in the nineteenth century held and propagated the view that no theory should exist if it did not produce dependency upon the Euro-supremacy mythology. In Gordon's opinion,[26] imperialist European historians discredited the work of African historians, such as the nineteenth-century precursors of Pan-Africanism, including Edward W. Blyden, Carl Christian Reindorf, Samuel Johnson and Joseph Isharam. Their historical work was regarded by European historians as the work of gifted and dedicated amateurs, but their work was not recognized by 'professional' historians and was little regarded in the universities and schools.[27] Consequently, the very idea of development as the offspring of the Enlightenment and modernity

---

23 Chukwuokolo, "Afrocentrism or Eurocentrism," 31.

24 Asante, *An Afrocentric Manifesto: Toward an African Renaissance*, 57.

25 Asante, *An Afrocentric Manifesto: Toward an African Renaissance*, 57.

26 Gordon, "Towards an African Historiography," 34.

27 Gordon, "Towards an African Historiography," 34.

became entangled in a complex and a long history mediated by the logic of coloniality informed by domination, oppression and exploitation. In addition, the rhetoric of modernity promised a brave modern society where salvation, civilization, progress, economic growth, freedom and democracy would be the order of life.[28]

In 1987, the then outgoing president of the Organization of American Historians, Leon Litwack, Professor of History at the University of California, Berkeley, criticized European scholars for their deliberate falsification and mythologizing of African history and culture. In his critique, he slated past historians for perpetuating racism and asked his present-day colleagues to try to heal that wound. He pointed out that 'no group of scholars was more deeply implicated in the miseducation of American youth and did more to shape the thinking of generations of Americans about race and Blacks than historians as they deliberately perpetuated racial stereotypes'. This accusation is explicit about the agenda of European scholarship to denigrate Africa and form false perceptions that in fact continue to sustain Euro-supremacist mythology. It is for this reason that even African scholars who suffered from intellectual dislocation as a result of their embeddedness in Eurocentrism continued to deny, during the 'Great Debate' of the 1970s and 1980s, that Africa had philosophy.[29]

According to Gordon, since 1947, there has been a revolution in African historiography.[30] He claims that the year 1947 marked the effective beginning of the modern movement, which led to the establishment of the University of Ibadan in Nigeria and the University of Ghana in 1948, and other institutions of higher learning throughout tropical Africa.[31] The new African universities had the blessing of Africans who had gone abroad to study in the United States, Great Britain, France and other European countries and in non-Western countries in the Caribbean. Scholars such as Kwame Nkrumah, Nnamdi Azikiwe, Jomo Kenyatta and Julius Nyerere began to challenge Western perceptions of Africans and African history.[32] For this reason, the retelling of African history from an African-centred perspective aims to debunk deliberate Eurocentric distortions. Thus, Asante suggests that the new Afrocentric historiography is not a false or artificial contrivance.[33]

---

28 Walter D. Mignolo, *The Idea of Latin America* (Malden, MA: Blackwell, 2005).

29 T. Uzodinma Nwala, *Critical Review of the Great Debate on African Philosophy (1970–1990)* (Ntsukka: William Amo Centre for African Philosophy UNN, 1992), 5.

30 Gordon, "Towards an African Historiography," 34.

31 Gordon, "Towards an African Historiography," 34.

32 Gordon, "Towards an African Historiography," 35.

33 Asante, *An Afrocentric Manifesto: Toward an African Renaissance*, 64.

Rather, it is a legitimate approach to the place of Africa in the world and the reassertion of African agency in pursuit of an African Renaissance. Out of an experience of great inquietude over a period of 500 years, Africans have now put into place, in the face of great resistance, the elements necessary for a truly African Renaissance founded on the principles and the centrality of African interests.[34]

Afrocentricity, as an intellectual *djed* grounded on centring Africans within their own historical and cultural experiences, provides a better perspective for an interpretation and understanding of African history that challenges African scholars to study history from the viewpoint of Africa and not of Europe. Afrocentricity insists that African people have a history, not one that is an appendage to European history, but one that antedates all other histories.[35] Keto attests that the Africa-centred perspective of history rests on the premise that it is valid to posit Africa as a geographical and cultural starting point in the study of peoples of African descent.[36] Thus, a non-hegemonic intellectual approach to the study of African history is not only significant for Africans but can also provide a better perspective for Europeans who seek to understand African ways of living.

Afrocentric Historiography and the Restoration of Africa's Contribution to World Civilization

As I have already indicated, Asante maintains that the emergence of the anti-African falsification has its origins in the rise of the European slave trade, because prior to the fifteenth century, Europeans had not yet formed the false logic of racial superiority and inferiority later used to justify negative ideas about Africa.[37] Adeleke[38] lauds two individuals for helping to advance the counterargument to this falsification: W. E. B. Du Bois and Carter G. Woodson. They strengthened the foundation upon which future generations, including Afrocentric scholars, would flourish. Thus, Afrocentric historicism emerged against the backdrop of the deliberate Eurocentric falsification and mythologization of Africa by European scholars as African intellectuals,

34 Asante, *An Afrocentric Manifesto: Toward an African Renaissance*, 7.

35 Don E. Luke, "Preserving the Euro-Supremacist Myth," in *Egypt vs. Greece and the American Academy: The Debate over the Birth of Civilization*, eds. Molefi Kete Asante and Ama Mazama (Chicago, IL: African American Images, 2002), 95.

36 C. Tsehloane Keto, *The African Centered Perspective of History* (Blackwood, NJ: K. A. Publications, 1989).

37 Asante, *Facing South to Africa*, 113.

38 Adeleke, "Africa and Afrocentric Historicism," 203.

borrowing from the past, began to invoke ancient African civilizations in their quest to counteract the Eurocentric narratives about African history. According to Adeleke, the preoccupation of black intellectuals with rewriting, revising and publicizing black history and culture became a critical repertoire of resistance.[39]

Monteiro-Ferreira explains that in the twentieth century, Africa's struggle for independence and self-determination came to embody a vast desire for liberation from oppressive colonial domination.[40] This quest was more than political; it included a call for economic, cultural and social agency because European modernity was the face of oppression. African intellectuals, therefore, by insisting on the need for an Afrocentric historical orientation in the spirit of a search for an African Renaissance opened the doors long held shut by Eurocentric orientations to phenomena.

The emergence of the field of Africology since the 1980s has enabled the development of innovative approaches to apprehending African phenomena as a restorative approach for the re-centring of Africans. Monteiro-Ferreira attests that 'the Western grand narratives, both mythological and historical, lost their omniscient truth in favour of the multiplicity of the different perspectives of non-hegemonic voices'.[41] One of the founders of Afrocentricity, Asante, emphasizes that Africology is sustained by the commitment to studying the life narratives, cultures, values and possibilities of the African people transnationally and transcontinentally.[42] One of the most important perspectives in this regard was the development of Afrocentricity as a locative paradigm.

Afrocentrists validate the work of Cheik Anta Diop, the Senegalese scholar, who wrote for the Negritudinists, as the precursor for the new Afrocentric historiography.[43] Asante[44] rates Diop the most significant African scholar of the century because of his demolition of the European construction of ancient Africa. Diop single-handedly, without African or European support, using melatonin studies and linguistic methods, established that the ancient Egyptians were black-skinned Africans and that the origin of civilization must be traced to the Nile Valley.[45] Asante and Mazama, the leading Afrocentrists

---

39 Adeleke, "Africa and Afrocentric Historicism," 201.

40 Monteiro-Ferreira, *The Demise of the Inhumane*, 37.

41 Monteiro-Ferreira, *The Demise of the Inhumane*, 332.

42 Asante, *African Pyramids of Knowledge*, 15.

43 Asante, *Facing South to Africa*; Diop, *The African Origin of Civilization*; Diop, *Civilization or Barbarism*.

44 Asante, *Facing South to Africa*, 13.

45 Asante, *Facing South to Africa*; Diop, *The African Origin of Civilization*; Diop, *Civilization or Barbarism*.

at Temple University, stress that Diop's argument overturns the Hegelian notion that Africa was outside history on the basis of Hegel's demonstrably false claim that African people did not have an historical consciousness.[46] Mazama saw in Diop's work 'a conscious elaboration of a paradigm whose main principle is the reclaiming of ancient Egypt, Kemet, for Africa'.[47] For this reason, Afrocentrists, citing Diop's research, argue that Kemet is to Africa what Greece is to Europe, and that a genuine African Renaissance must be grounded on the fertile soil of the Nile Valley Civilization, as Diop argues.[48] The Nile Valley Civilization, which arose about 3400 BCE in historical terms and ended with the Roman dispossession around 50 BCE, did not evolve in isolation from the rest of Africa. Egypt was clearly an African civilization and was connected to Africa's history and geography, just as ancient Nubia was.[49] Therefore, robbing Africans of their account of history is nothing less than a campaign designed to destroy their civilization and promote unfair intellectualism among European scholars who attempt to falsify African history.

Africans, like other human beings, are products of the environment. Gordon argues that the geographic base of Africa provides a background for understanding the genesis of humankind and the origins of agriculture in Africa, as well as the rise and fall of African kingdoms, the world of the desert and African trade with the outside world.[50,51] For this reason, the understanding of Africa's geographical location has a great impact on any understanding of African ways of life; hence, African history must be told from the African standpoint.

Asante calls for '[t]he anteriority of the classical African civilizations [to] be entertained in any Africological inquiry', adding that '[c]lassical references are necessary as a baseline frame for discussing the development of African cultural phenomena'.[52] Asante also maintains that 'a new revolutionary moment in which African people interrogate and locate within their own history the values, concepts, and ideals that are essential

---

46 Asante, *An Afrocentric Manifesto: Toward an African Renaissance*, 13.

47 Asante, *An Afrocentric Manifesto: Toward an African Renaissance*, 13.

48 Cited in Asante, *An Afrocentric Manifesto: Toward an African Renaissance*, 69.

49 Molefi Kete Asante, "Locating the Eurocentric Assumptions about African History," in *Egypt vs. Greece and the American Academy: The Debate over the Birth of Civilization*, eds. Molefi Kete Asante and Ama Mazama (Chicago, IL: African American Images, 2002), 11.

50 Gordon, "Towards an African Historiography," 28.

51 Diop, *The African Origin of Civilization*; Diop, *Civilization or Barbarism*.

52 Asante, *African Pyramids of Knowledge*, 15.

for a reinvigorated society can be advanced by seriously engaging the Nile Valley civilizations'.[53]

Thus, the research on classical African history produced by Diop, Martin Bernal, Du Bois, George G. M. James and many other African scholars remains relevant and critical in laying the foundations for understanding African history. The Diopian view of historiography combines research on linguistics, history and psychology to interpret the cultural unity of the African people.[54] The summation of Diop's argument is that the ancient Egyptians were black-skinned Africans and that the origin of civilization must be traced to the Nile Valley. As Diop indicates in his introduction to *Civilization or Barbarism: An Authentic Anthropology*, his final and most powerful work, his theory of the African origin of civilization is grounded in the idea that all cultures have a continuity that can be traced back to an African origin.[55] Thus, Diop's concern with the African origin of civilization is related to the modern idea of Afrocentricity, which includes, but is not limited to, the discourse around the origin of civilization.[56]

According to Asante, 'Diop reconstructed an approach to an understanding of African history that unsettled the vast circles of traditional European thought, including African scholars who are rooted within the Eurocentric paradigm'.[57] It was this principle that agitated Western scholars and created an avalanche of criticism of Diop's work and Afrocentricity. Winters[58] affirms Asante's position that the critique of many Eurocentric scholars to Afrocentricity results from aggressive white resistance to Diop's idea of a black Egypt and the view that Egyptians spoke an African language, rather than an Afro-Asiatic language. Karenga[59] also endorses the Diopian historiography by stating that Kemet (Egypt) is the source of an African Renaissance because the position it holds is unquestioned as the source of the energy behind the expansion of African ideas that have held Africans together in a unique historical situation.

---

53 Asante, *An Afrocentric Manifesto: Toward an African Renaissance*, 69.

54 Clyde A. Winters, "Ancient Afrocentric History and the Genetic Model," in *Egypt vs. Greece and the American Academy: The Debate over the Birth of Civilization*, eds. Molefi Kete Asante and Ama Mazama (Chicago, IL: African American Images, 2002), 121–64.

55 Diop, *Civilization or Barbarism*.

56 Charles C. Verharen, "In and Out of Africa: Misreading Afrocentricity," in *Egypt vs. Greece and the American Academy: The Debate over the Birth of Civilization*, ed. Molefi Kete Asante and Ama Mazama (Chicago, IL: African American Images, 2002), 70.

57 Asante, *An Afrocentric Manifesto: Toward an African Renaissance*, 13.

58 Winters, "Ancient Afrocentric History," 121.

59 Maulana Karenga, *Maat: The Moral Ideal in Ancient Egypt* (Los Angeles, CA: University of Sankore Press, 2006).

The reason Kemet still creates interest among many African scholars is that it established its own will over a long period and has shaped succeeding civilizations with its profound discoveries.[60] For this reason, it is crucial to state that what Europe had succeeded in doing to Africa and Africans since the rise of modern Europe to power was to dethrone Africans from their own agency, self-assertion and cultural definition based on Africa's own historical development, turning the continent's people into a beggar people.[61] Indeed, the African paradox since the colonial invasion is that Africa remains the continent with the most riches, yet with its people are the poorest in the world. Asante maintains that 'a new revolutionary moment in which African people interrogate and locate within their own history the values, concepts, and ideals that are essential for a reinvigorated society can be advanced by seriously engaging the Nile Valley civilizations'.[62]

Given that most European historians in the nineteenth century sought to sustain the false idea of Egyptians as white or Mediterranean in line with their political agenda, it remains necessary to revisit historical facts to reassert the blackness of ancient Africans. According to Winters,[63] many European scholars who mention the work of Diop in their articles have never reviewed his work properly because they seem to lack the ability to understand the many disciplines that Diop mastered. Diop earned his PhD in Egyptology from the Sorbonne University in Paris.[64] During his higher education, he conducted formal studies and gained practical experience with some of the great physicists and chemists of Europe, and later directed the radiocarbon dating laboratory in Dakar, Senegal. Moreover, Diop was trained in anthropology and was a linguist of note.[65] Diop, with all his achievements, became an unparalleled expert in the study of Kemet and Greece. For this reason, it is surprising that Euro-supremacist scholars denigrated his knowledge and disregarded his work as being worth considering in the study and understanding of Africa.

One of the Eurocentric scholars who has criticized Diop's work without providing any evidence based on a thorough interrogation of his work is

60 Asante, *An Afrocentric Manifesto: Toward an African Renaissance*, 70.

61 Asante, *An Afrocentric Manifesto: Toward an African Renaissance*, 56.

62 Asante, *An Afrocentric Manifesto: Toward an African Renaissance*, 69.

63 Winters, "Ancient Afrocentric History," 122.

64 Asa G. Hilliard III, "The Myth of the Immaculate Conception of Western Civilization," in *Egypt vs. Greece and the American Academy: The Debate over the Birth of Civilization*, ed. Molefi Kete Asante and Ama Mazama (Chicago, IL: African American Images, 2002) 63.

65 Hilliard, "The Myth of the Immaculate Conception."

Lefkowitz.[66] She rejects Diop's argument that ancient Egyptians were black in her book *Not Out of Africa*[67] without presenting tangible evidence to counter Diop's work or even using the work published by other scholars to prove Diop is incorrect in his analysis.[68] Lefkowitz rejects Diop's work by claiming that 'his research is not so thorough as it might appear'; she further criticizes Diop by stating that his work relied on only one source and has uncritically repeated an ancient claim of 'dubious accuracy'.[69] Another critic is Baines, who in the *New York Times Book Review* did the most popular review of Diop's work.[70] As with Lefkowitz's criticism of Diop's work, Baines also fails to substantiate his opinion and merely criticizes Diop's work by labelling it 'unsound'.[71] Winters argues that their criticism is not sufficiently professional to carry weight[72] and that, in academia, to refute a thesis, one must present counter-evidence that disproves the logic of the thesis under review and cannot rely on unsubstantiated rhetoric. This shows the simplistic manner in many Euro-supremacist scholars' style of argumentation used to dismiss African scholars to maintain their false supremacy.

A revered African American scholar who, like Diop, has challenged the idea that Greeks were the authors of philosophy and science is George G. M. James, with his 1954 book, *Stolen Legacy: The Greeks Were Not the Authors of Greek Philosophy, but the People of North Africa*.[73] James sought to prove that Greek civilization was influenced by Egyptian civilization, not the other way around. Asante affirms that 'from this vantage point it was easier for those who came after James to examine his arguments and to use them in their own redemptive work'.[74] Other scholars such as John Henrik Clarke, Ivan Van Sertima, Yosef ben-Jochannan, Jacob Carruthers, Wade Nobles and Asa G. Hilliard III have used James's work with great benefit to their readers as well.[75] James argues that the Egyptians, as black Africans, produced the arguments, knowledge, evidence and theories upon which Greek civilization, which was to come thousands of years later, would depend.[76]

66 Winters, "Ancient Afrocentric History."

67 Lefkowitz, *Not Out of Africa*.

68 Winters, "Ancient Afrocentric History."

69 Lefkowitz, *Not Out of Africa*, 17.

70 John Baines, "Was Civilization Made in Africa?" *The New York Times Review of Books*, 1 (August 1, 1991):12–13.

71 Baines, "Was Civilization Made in Africa?"

72 Winters, "Ancient Afrocentric History," 122.

73 James, *Stolen Legacy*.

74 Asante, *Facing South to Africa*, 13.

75 Asante, *Facing South to Africa*.

76 Asante, *Facing South to Africa*, 14; George G. M. James, *Stolen Legacy* (New York, NY: Classic House Books, [1954] 2009).

Finch corroborates that the Nile Valley high culture was already complete and mature by 4000 BCE and remained an intact and powerful force for the next four millennia.[77] Thus, Egypt stood out as the political overlord of most of the Eastern half of the Mediterranean and, even when Egypt was not in political control, its cultural hegemony was paramount.[78] Asante contends that Egypt is far older as a civilization of thinkers than Greece[79] because Egypt predates Greece in political terms, its development of science, method, theory and philosophy.[80] The ancient Nile Valley thinkers contributed to the world a full body of intellectual and creative works long before Thales, Anaximander and Anaximenes of Miletus and Heraclitus of Ephesus, or Isocrates the Ionian came to study with them in the sixth century BCE.[81] Obenga notes that Thales, considered to be the father of Greek philosophy, received his education in Egypt and was trained by Egyptian priests.[82] Having received instruction on the method of studying, the nature of things and of truth in Egypt, Thales went back to his native city of Miletus as an elder, with knowledge and wisdom.[83] The Greek philosopher Plato (428–347 BCE) is recorded as stating that 'Thales was educated in Egypt under the priests'.[84] For this reason, to many Afrocentrists, it is surprising that modern European scholars deliberately omit such details, and as a result continue to falsify African knowledge and contributions to the foundation of Greek civilization.

Besides African contributions in philosophy and science, Karenga contends that Africans contributed significantly to the ideals of an ethical and just society by introducing the concept of *Maat*.[85] According to Karenga, the concept of *Maat* is derived from a physical concept of straightness, evenness and levelness.[86] Thus, *Maat* came to be identified with the pursuit for truth, righteousness, justice, order, balance, harmony and reciprocity. Through the concept of

77 Charles Finch III, "Critiquing the Critics: Advancing the Paradigm," in *Egypt vs. Greece and the American Academy: The Debate over the Birth of Civilization*, edited by Molefi Kete Asante and Ama Mazama (Chicago, IL: African American Images, 2002), 38.

78 Finch, "Critiquing the Critics."

79 Molefi Kete Asante, *The Egyptian Philosophers: Ancient African Voices from Imhotep to Akhenaten* (Chicago, IL: African American Images, 2000).

80 Asante, *The Egyptian Philosophers.*

81 Asante, *The Egyptian Philosophers*, viii.

82 Theophile Obenga, "Thales of Miletus and Egypt," in *Egypt vs. Greece and the American Academy: The Debate over the Birth of Civilization*, eds. Molefi Kete Asante and Ama Mazama (Chicago, IL: African American Images, 2002), 167.

83 Obenga, "Thales of Miletus and Egypt," 168.

84 Plato. [ca 375 BCE] *The Republic*, X, 600A.

85 Karenga, *Maat: The Moral Ideal.*

86 Karenga, *Maat: The Moral Ideal.*

Maat, a society founded on the ideals of peace, harmony and justice could be established. Asante maintains that African history is rich with philosophical concepts in search of *Maat*, even if it is often called by different names, and is taught by sage philosophers in the villages: 'This concept corresponds to certain aspects of Dja, Iwa or Ubuntu in various parts of Africa.'[87]

Regarding architecture, Finch rightly reminds us that Egypt was the first to raise massively precise edifices in stone,[88] elaborating monumental architectural styles whose influences would eventually be felt as far away as Mexico. The so-called 'Doric' column had already achieved perfection of form by the 3rd Dynasty, more than 3000 years before the building of the Parthenon.[89] How could it then be that Eurocentric scholars fail to acknowledge these grand achievements unless their motive is self-enlargement through deliberate attempts to falsify knowledge? The European historians of the nineteenth century generally discredited *African* contributions to civilization in a bid to deny Africans their rightful and deserving respect. Much evidence abounds that the Egyptians were great; for example, Finch points out that in astronomy, almost every Greek writer who mentions the subject traces the origin of scientific astronomy to Egypt and Chaldea, through giving priority to Egypt:

> Ancient Egyptians developed no fewer than three calendars: lunar, Sirian-solar, and precessional. The precessional calendar is derived from the retrograde movement of the celestial North Pole around the ecliptic North Pole, encompassing the period of 26,000 years. The Sirian solar calendar is based on the difference between the true year of 365 determined by heliacal rising of Sirius at the summer solstice and the civil calendar conventionalized at 365 days. In the late antiquity, at the insistence of first the Ptolemies, then Julius Caesar, the calendrists of Kemet devised a leap year to reconcile the two calendars.[90]

Besides astronomy, it is also to the Nile Valley that we must look for evidence of early influences on Greek mathematics. Finch maintains that the geometry of Pythagoras, Eudoxus, Plato and Euclid was learned in the Nile Valley temples.[91] Four mathematical papyri still survive, most importantly the Rhind

87 Asante, *Facing South to Africa*, 21.
88 Finch, "Critiquing the Critics," 38.
89 Finch, "Critiquing the Critics," 38.
90 Finch, "Critiquing the Critics," 39.
91 Finch, "Critiquing the Critics."

mathematical papyrus dating to 1832 BCE. With so much evidence abounding about Egyptian influence on Greek civilization, European scholars' elevation of the Greeks without giving sufficient credit to the ancient Egyptians (as Africans) does not hold water. These scholars falsely created an impression that ancient Greek civilization was a product of an 'immaculate conception' untouched by any influence from their Kemet neighbours.

With modern-day Afrocentric scholars exposing the false logic of an African history rooted in Eurocentrism, the monumental challenge facing African scholars is to retell the African tale in pursuit of an African Renaissance. According to Asante, the issue during the last half of the twentieth century seems to be addressing the following question: 'Now that African nations are independent and African peoples throughout the world are gaining freedom from oppression, humiliation, degradation and inequality, what are the missing pages in the book of African redemption?'[92] Ndlovu-Gatsheni[93] puts it slightly differently, as I have already noted, asking what the search for African development means for people who are struggling to emerge and free themselves from the legacies of enslavement, colonialism, imperialism, apartheid, neocolonialism, underdevelopment and the imposition of the Washington Consensus of 1989 and neoliberalism.

To respond to both Asante and Ndlovu-Gatsheni's questions, it needs to be clear that it would be impossible and indeed pointless for Africa to attempt to imitate any idea of development or advancement outside of its own history and cultural paradigm, as this would be a continuation of Africans' dislocation. Without a doubt, Africa must find itself based on its own terms and insist on its own agency for its own renaissance. The answers for a resurgence of Africa lie in a re-centring of Africans in their own historical and cultural terms, to end the dismemberment engineered by the Scramble for Africa that culminated in the Berlin Conference, which physically partitioned the continent, but also wrecked the psychological make-up of Africans by reducing them to recipients of the purported 'salvation' of an imposed European identity. Therefore, the only hope for Africans in a world hegemonized by a colonial lineage (both Arabic and European) is for Africans to find their own roots and be relocated to their own centre and terms. From that centre, they will be able to correctly understand their own identity and fulfil their destiny: the establishment of identity determines activity. For this reason, Afrocentricity aims to revive an African consciousness grounded on African history and culture to end Africa's alienation from itself by the European invasion.

---

92 Asante, *An Afrocentric Manifesto: Toward an African Renaissance*, 55.
93 Ndlovu-Gatsheni, "The African Idea of Development," 1.

The African Renaissance and the African Development Challenge in Post-colonial Africa

Cheikh Anta Diop popularized the concept of what he called an African Renaissance in the mid-1940s when he drew attention to the significance of anchoring African development in African history and African culture, as well as the importance of mobilizing Africans on the continent and in the diaspora to take charge of creating their own futures.[94] Asante[95] reminds us that Diop was born in the colonial era and was educated in schools established by colonial teachers, and yet he would read the documents of Western culture with two sets of notes, one for the examination and another for his personal sanity. This great African scholar knew that the only way for Africa to rise again was through a revival rooted in Africa's historical past and not in its imputed (false) colonial identity.

The concept of the African Renaissance eventually became a viable tool to debate the need for the intellectual relocation of Africans from Eurocentric intellectual imprisonment into the streams of their historical journey and culture. Since Africans have been removed from their own terms culturally, psychologically, economically, politically and historically, it is essential for any assessment going forward of the African condition to be made from the African location.[96] This means that all analysis of African phenomena needs to be seen in the light of Africans as actors and not as mere spectators and mimics of Europe. Thus, Afrocentricity, as a paradigm that seeks the resurgence of Africans, establishes the intellectual location for the interpretation of African phenomena. The intellectual location in this context speaks to the psychological and historical space occupied by an observer of phenomena.[97]

The African Renaissance as a Pan-African concept sets Africans on a trajectory towards their own liberation by restoring their memories of how they came to be disrupted from their destiny. According to Asante, the Dakar meeting of African intellectuals called by President Wade of Senegal in December 2003 was the most historic congress on the African continent.[98] The congress brought African intellectuals from Africa, the Caribbean and the Americas together to contemplate an African Renaissance. Now that Africa had become politically independent, it was necessary for intellectuals

94 Ndlovu-Gatsheni, Sabelo J., "Revisiting the African Renaissance," in *Oxford Research Encyclopedia* (Oxford: Oxford University Press, 2019), 28.

95 Asante, *Facing South to Africa*, 79.

96 Asante, *An Afrocentric Manifesto: Toward an African Renaissance*, 31.

97 Asante, "Locating the Eurocentric Assumptions."

98 Asante, *An Afrocentric Manifesto: Toward an African Renaissance*, 55.

to help deepen the epistemological decolonization necessary for the relocation of African minds from Europe. The implication of this is that it is not enough only to remember an Africa that was colonized by Europeans – we need to transcend the painful memory and integrate the whole of Africa, beginning with the Nile Valley Civilization, Africa East, West and South and hold Africa as one with all its invention.

The renaissance of Africa therefore needs to begin with the idea that Africa must never participate in its own demise and must escape all conceptual imprisonment created by European colonialists. This also implies that African conceptions of development be moved out from under the European lens and cultural practices to Afrocentric lenses to enable relevance. Thus, the moral aesthetics of Afrocentricity as a guiding theoretical frame in this study is that it situates Africans in the centre of the African narratives of place and time, demonstrating that the dislocation of Africans from the centre of their own history is a form of intellectual and cultural terrorism that maintains its constant attack on the African concept of self and idea of time.[99] As a result of colonialism, Africans live through terms defined by someone else and not by themselves, which means they are dislocated from their own social reality. Hence, Afrocentricity advances the idea that the resurgence of Africa can only happen when Africans are grounded in the philosophical soil of African history, without this there can be no African Renaissance nor any meaningful future for Africans . Asante (2018:8) affirms that 'Africans cannot be future oriented if they cannot conceive of themselves as subjects and agents responsible for their own freedom'.

African Renaissance is about the quest for wholeness in the aftermath of what the Berlin Conference of 1884/5 did to cut Africa into 54 colonies (now independent nation-states) that continue to be the surrogates of European colonialists, even in the aftermath of independence. Kwame Nkrumah correctly uses the term *neocolonialism*[100] in his description of the state of capture that African states continue to suffer in the post-independence era. Ngugi wa Thiong'o (2009a:28) describes the dismemberment of Africa as a 'colonial act',[101] a 'practice of power, intended to pacify a populace, and a symbolic act, a performance of power intended to produce docile minds'. Moreover, dismemberment is also an act of absolute social engineering; thus, the dismembering of Africa was the foundation on which Europe's capitalist

99 Asante, *Facing South to Africa*.

100 Nkrumah, *Neo-Colonialism*.

101 Ngugi wa Thiong'o, *Something Torn and New*, 28. Ngugi wa Thiong'o, *Re-membering Africa*, 28.

economy was established (Ngugi wa Thiong'o, 2009:28).[102] Therefore, the renaissance of Africa needs to be mapped as a restorative trajectory aimed at curing the sociopolitical and economic ills created through colonialism and neocolonialism and to bind up the hurts and pains that the continent of Africa suffered and continues to suffer.

In 1997, Thabo Mbeki delivered a lengthy speech in the United States where he posited that 'the African Renaissance is upon us', and elaborated as follows: 'This generation remains African and carries with it an historic pride which compels for Africans to be seen as equal to all the other peoples of our common universe.'[103] Without a doubt, Mbeki struck the correct chord by emphasizing the need for Africa to be self-dependent as the main strategy for Africa's resurgence from oppression. Like Mbeki, Asante[104] points out that Africa possesses its own rich heritage of intellectual ideas, and these ideas must be mined for the proper and correct gems for the future of the African Renaissance. Thus, Afrocentricity as an intellectual *djed* affirms the significance of centring Africans within their own history as a compass leading them to the streams of their eternal glory. For this reason, any notion of African development that does not advance the interests of the African people remains a hegemonic strategy to continue the subjugation of African people.

Asante, through the idea of Afrocentricity, emphasizes that we cannot understand Africa's contribution to its own development and the world at large without examining the basis for society – the history, culture and values that make up that society.[105] Undoubtedly, history is significant in the narrative of societal advancement, but what is more important is *who* provides the historical narrative of Africa and *for what agenda*. The history of Africa told by Europeans only serves the purpose of glorifying Europe as the centre of Africa. It is for this reason that the post–World War II articulation of how Africa should advance itself in pursuit of its future glorified the idea of European modernization, which encouraged Africa to imitate European experiences. Such an idea must be rejected because it locates African development within the epistemic foundations of European history and experiences and further dislocates Africans from their own history. The implication of this insight is awareness

102 Ngugi wa Thiong'o, *Something Torn and New*, 28. Ngugi wa Thiong'o, *Re-membering Africa*, 28.

103 Thabo Mbeki, "Address by Executive Deputy President Thabo Mbeki, to Corporate Council on Africa's 'Attracting Capital' Summit," Chantilly VA, 19–22 April 1997, South African History Online, http://www.dirco.gov.za, 1.

104 Asante, *Facing South to Africa*, 101.

105 Asante, *An Afrocentric Manifesto: Toward an African Renaissance*, 66.

of the fact that the Truman version of development after 1945 was interwoven with Western triumphalist declarations and acts, which eroded the possibility for Africans to rise. It was nothing but another 'imperial project' as Cheru points out,[106] because this articulation was rooted in the long history of Europe's mission to conquer Africa, as expressed in the comments on Africa by European thinkers such as Hegel, Hume, Trevor-Roper, Weber and many others. This idea of development remains the offspring of the Enlightenment and modernity and is entangled in a complex European history mediated through the logics of 'neocolonialism'.[107]

African revitalization lies in the ability of Africans themselves to transcend the narrow Eurocentric constructions and reclaim their own definitions not shaped after European thoughts, but their own. In the spirit of raising the bar of the African Renaissance, Asante raises the following fundamental questions: 'Who is to say that the historical experiences of the African world are less valid for Africans than others? What resonates more than the centrality of Africans to their own history, not someone else's?'[108]

In the light of 500 years of European physical, political, economic and epistemic domination of Africans, it can only be noble for Africans to seize power to define their destiny. Hence, Ndlovu-Gatsheni[109] invokes Ngugi wa Thiong'o's idea of 're-membering'[110] in his reflections on the African development challenge when he states that 'African conceptions of development continue to be a struggle for the remembering of the continent', that is, the quest for wholeness after over five centuries of 'dismemberment'.

Ndlovu-Gatsheni's article 'Revisiting the African Renaissance' (2019) articulates what he considers to be the five moments of contemporary African history and politics that have framed the struggle for African Renaissance. In his view, the first moment was formed by the seventeenth-century struggle for political decolonization in Haiti, which Kwame Nkrumah in the twentieth century expresses as the seeking of a 'political kingdom'.[111] This moment was exemplified by the historic struggle that led to the establishment of the first 'black republic' through the Haitian Revolution (1791–1804). Both Asante[112] and Ndlovu-Gatsheni[113] regard the Haitian Revolution

106 Cheru, "Development in Africa."
107 Nkrumah, *Neo-Colonialism.*
108 Asante, *An Afrocentric Manifesto: Toward an African Renaissance*, 25.
109 Ndlovu-Gatsheni, "The African Idea of Development," 2.
110 Ngugi wa Thiong'o, *Re-membering Africa.*
111 Nkrumah, *Neo-Colonialism.*
112 Asante, *Facing South to Africa*, 60.
113 Ndlovu-Gatsheni, "Revisiting the African Renaissance," 7.

as exemplifying the struggle of African people to break away from a racist Western oppressive regime in search of their freedom to self-govern. After the Haitian Revolution, we witnessed the rise of Pan-Africanism in the early 1900s as a basis for an African awakening to political decolonization globally. The movement was advanced strongly by the brilliant leadership of thinkers such as W. E. B. Du Bois and Marcus Garvey, despite their strategic differences, what was clear was the fact that they led the Pan-African desire for African liberation.

Ndlovu-Gatsheni[114] sees the second moment that fortified the search and calls for an African Renaissance in the call for economic decolonization and in addressing what Kwame Nkrumah of Ghana termed 'neocolonialism'.[115] According to Nkrumah, neocolonialism describes the subtle state of capture in which Western colonial empires continue to exercise indirect control over their former African colonies, through trade agreements, as a strategy to ensure that they never become economically independent.[116] Thus, it became significant for African leaders to devise strategies for economic renewal to ensure that they could escape from economic dependence on their former colonizers. Political decolonization that is not underpinned by economic decolonization means that independent African countries will continue to remain tied to the manoeuvres of Western empires, thus failing to break free from colonial bondage. For this reason, both political and economic decolonization struggles were and still are intertwined with African decolonization projects.

Ndlovu-Gatsheni[117] regards the third moment of the crystallization of the African Renaissance in the post-colonial struggles for popular democracy, ranged against long-standing single party and military dictatorships, as well as opposition to the International Monetary Fund and World Bank austerity measures of the Structural Adjustment Programmes which have created the debt dependency of African states. African leaders, in the spirit of an African Renaissance, created counter-hegemonic development initiatives to challenge the Western powers. Although most of their initiatives were disrupted and undermined by the neocolonial forces, Africans never gave up. For example, to mention only a few, their initiatives included the *African Declaration on Cooperation, Development and Economic Independence* of 1973, the *Revised Framework of the Principles for the Implementation of the New International*

114 Ndlovu-Gatsheni, "Revisiting the African Renaissance," 10.
115 Nkrumah, *Neo-Colonialism.*
116 Nkrumah, *Neo-Colonialism.*
117 Ndlovu-Gatsheni, "Revisiting the African Renaissance," 12.

Economic Order in Africa of 1976, the *Lagos Plan of Action for the Economic Development of Africa* of 1980, the *African Priority Programme for Economic Recovery* of 1986, the *African Charter for Popular Participation for Development* of 1990, the United Nations' *New Agenda for Development of Africa* of 1991 and the *New Partnership for African Development* (*NEPAD*) of 2001.[118]

Lastly, yet importantly in his outline, Ndlovu-Gatsheni mentions two major moments which are significant for the African Renaissance, namely the Afro-Arab Spring and the #Rhodes Must Fall movements.[119]

The Afro-Arab Spring movement, which broke out in 2011, targeted the long-standing dictatorial regimes in Tunisia, Egypt and Libya, which had survived the second and third waves of democratization that engulfed sub-Saharan Africa in the late 1980s and early 1990s.[120] His hopeful view is undercut by Villa-Vicencio, Doxtader and Moosa, who liken the North African revolutionary movements to the spring season and argue that the mere change of a 'season' is not enough to amount to a renaissance[121]; in their view, spring is but a fragile season. This implies that these countries need to go beyond the mere change of a political season and that the movement must mature into more strategic political change that will lead to a true democratic mass revolution.

The #Rhodes Must Fall movements which began in South Africa in 2015 involved a call for epistemological decolonization. Students demanded that they be taught the relevant educational content that correctly portrays Africa's achievements in world civilization and not Africa as a dependent of Europe. Thus, the demand for epistemological decolonization was about dismantling the colonial epistemic empire and elevating African native intelligence, with an aim to correct the injustices committed by colonial epistemicides. Hence, the demand for epistemological decolonization advanced the critical need to ensure that the education system for Africans centre Africans within their own historical context and liberate them from epistemic dependence on Eurocentrism.

---

118 Cited in Jimi O. Adesina, Yao Graham, and Adebayo O. Olukoshi, *Africa and Development Challenges in the New Millennium: The NEPAD Debate* (London: Zed Books, 2006).

119 Ndlovu-Gatsheni, "Revisiting the African Renaissance," 18.

120 Ndlovu-Gatsheni, "Revisiting the African Renaissance," 18.

121 Charles Villa-Vicencio, Erik Doxtader, and Ebrahim Moosa, *The African Renaissance and the Afro-Arab Spring: A Season of Rebirth?* (Cape Town: University of Cape Town Press, 2015).

Chapter 5

AFROCENTRICITY ON THE SIGNIFICANCE OF CULTURE IN THE CONCEPTUALIZATION OF AN AFRICAN DEVELOPMENT PARADIGM

Culture stands out as a critical aspect of Afrocentricity in terms of an analysis of what should inform the Afrocentric development trajectory in Africa and for Africans in the diaspora. The European invasion of Africa set in motion cultural imperialism that resulted in the dislocation of African people from their own cultural grounding.

As I have mentioned in Chapter 3, the discourse of development in Africa has remained deeply entangled in colonially imposed matrices of power.[1,2] It has not enabled Africans to imagine development from the perspective of their own history and cultural experiences. Such a perspective on development has only imposed on Africa a tendency to mimic the European modernization project as the sole model that should define what development is for Africa because the conceptualization of mainstream development in the aftermath of World War II was guided by modernization theory, with its extension as a neoliberal framework derived from the experiences of Western countries.

The main challenge facing Africa since the fifteenth century, which marks the start of mercantilism and Christianization, is the need for Africans to find their own voices and a cultural anchor for their endeavour to shape Africa's development prospects. Epistemic colonization by European scholars produced a continent dependent on Europeans to define the value of African's culture, including what that culture meant for the development future of Africa. Their agenda was to create Africans who think from a European perspective and who will forever remain dependent beneficiaries of Europe. Marimba Ani in her book *Yuguru: An Afrikan-Centered Critique of European Cultural Thought and*

1 Ndlovu-Gatsheni, "The Entrapment of Africa."

2 Quijano, "The Coloniality of Power."

Behaviour, therefore, attacks European cultural imperialism in her reference to the concept of *asili*, the central seed or germinating matrix of a culture, to expose how European white supremacist thought believes in its own superiority to the denigration of African culture and humanity.[3] As a result of the Eurocentrism of development discourse, African development discourse has for too long accepted the idea of the 'catch-up thesis', as Mkandawire calls it,[4] which presents the development in Africa as seeking to be like the West – industrialized and modern. This is a trend which, in Afrocentric terms, we refer to as a cultural imperialist venture, and which must be resisted.

In order to redefine what the process of development should entail for Africa, deliberations must be grounded on African culture as a basis to illuminate relevant development theorization. For this reason, Afrocentricity, the guiding theoretical framework for this book, insists on the significance of the particularity of a context defined by time and space as the starting point from which to understand the making, unmaking and remaking of an African society. In particular, this paradigm emphasizes the significance of relocating African people to their own cultural roots as the centre from which to interpret their reality. Asante believes that without a plausible ideology, we as Africans can never march in the same direction.[5] Afrocentricity is therefore essential for the attainment of a collective African development vision.

If we ignore the cultural context from which we speak when we analyse a phenomenon, we become dislocated in our understanding and thought process. Thus, development in Africa, grounded on the ideals of Afrocentricity, must ensure that Africans are the agents of their own development, as opposed to being viewed as dependent beneficiaries of European-designed development experiments. Our development vision must be informed by African history and cultural practices – relying on anything outside of African experiences becomes a hegemonic enterprise. Bruton[6] notes that 'knowledge about the development process in a particular time does not exist in transferable form, rather it is a product of the development process itself'. This chapter rearticulates the question of development as inextricably intertwined with the question of culture. Cultural imperialism as an important technology of underdeveloping Africa needs to be addressed to resolve the current development impasse.

---

3 Marimba Ani, *Yuguru: An Afrikan-centered Critique of European Cultural Thought and Behaviour* (Trenton, NJ: Africa World Press, 1994).

4 Mkandawire, "Running While Others Walk," 13.

5 Asante, *African Pyramids of Knowledge*, vii.

6 Bruton, Henry J., "The Search for a Development Economics," *World Development* 13, nos. 10–11 (1985): 1099–1124, also cited in Brohman, "Universalism, Eurocentrism," 121.

European colonization of Africa ushered in European cultural dominance, which remodelled the continent to push it towards imbibing a Western way of life, and thus made Africa's political, economic and social development aspirations conform to European (and thus foreign) ways of life. It is no wonder that such development projects had little success in Africa, since they were rooted in the idea of a European modernization of Africa. The primary argument advanced in this book, and in this chapter, is that Africans must relocate to their own cultural terms and must be the subject and not the object of (European) cultural imperialism. African cultural regeneration is projected as the starting point and solution for the liberation of the continent from Western domination. Mbakogu points out that

> [c]ulture plays an invisible role in determining our customs, values, morals and growth in society, and that if we truly aspire freedom from the shackles of underdevelopment, there is an urgent need to break away from the confines of Western cultural systems and search for that which made us Africans prior to colonization.[7]

No human exists outside of culture. Rather, we are inheritors and conveyors of culture. Culture informs the meaning we give to life, and it determines our activities in pursuit of our destinies.

Defining the Concept of Culture

The concept of culture connotes different things to different individuals and has been defined differently by many scholars. However, although there are probably as many definitions of culture as there are writers, most definitions have a number of elements in common. For Asante and the circle of Afrocentric scholars, 'the useful way to view the cultural question Afrocentrically lies in the understanding of "culture as shared perceptions, attitudes, and predispositions that allow people to organize experiences in certain ways"'.[8]

The culture of a people is what distinguishes them from other societies in the family of humanity. Culture, as it is understood from an Afrocentric perspective, entails a totality of traits and characters that are peculiar to a people to the extent that it marks them out from other peoples or societies. These peculiar traits include a people's language, dress, music, work, arts,

7 Ifeyinwa Annastasia Mbakogu, "Is There Really a Relationship Between Culture and Development?" *Anthropology* 6, no. 1 (2004): 42.

8 Asante, *Kemet, Afrocentricity, and Knowledge*, 9.

religion, dancing and so on. Other scholars who are not necessarily part of the Afrocentric circle led by Asante have also shed some light on the concept of culture, which affirms the views expressed by Temple Circle of Afrocentric scholarship. For example, Aziza (2001:31) defines culture as follows:

> Culture is the totality of the pattern of behaviour of a particular group of people. It includes everything that makes them distinct from any other group of people, for instance, their greeting habits, dressing, social norms and taboos, food, songs and dance patterns, rites of passages from birth, through marriage to death, traditional occupations, religious as well as philosophical beliefs.[9]

Idang (2015) is another scholar who divides culture into its material and non-material aspects.[10] For him, the material aspects of culture refer to the visible tactile objects which humans are able to manufacture for the purpose of survival in their environment, such as artefacts and crafts, while non-material aspects entail beliefs, values, attitudes and general behaviours that shape the course of people's lives (Idang, 2015:100).[11]

In a nutshell, culture is a network of traits that are learned, based on interaction or derived from history. Culture is passed from one generation to the next generation, and it is a by-product of the socialization process. Therefore, the idea of African culture, as defined by Ezedike,[12] refers to the sum of the shared attitudinal inclinations and capabilities, art, beliefs, moral codes and practices that characterize Africans. It can be conceived of as a continuous, cumulative reservoir containing both material and non-material elements that are socially transmitted from one generation to another. African culture, therefore, refers to the entire African heritage. Thus, human behaviour, value systems, attitudes and practices are all cultural expressions, as no human in the world exists outside of culture or without culture.

That said, it can be inferred that culture is the pride of every society; it regulates our lives consciously or unconsciously. These reflections on culture challenge the incorrect postulations made by Hegel in his 1828 lectures on history, when he pronounced that 'Africa must be forgotten because it was no part of history and had no culture'.[13] Hegel, like many other European

---

9 Aziza

10 Idang

11 Idang

12 E. O. Ezedike, *African Culture and the African Personality. From Footmarks to Landmarks on African Philosophy* (Somolu: Obaroh and Ogbinaka Publishers, 2009), 455.

13 Cited in Asante, *Facing South to Africa*, 115.

historians, was influenced by and promoted racist scholarship which portrayed Africa in a negative light in support of European conquest. Asante points out that when King Leopold of Belgium declared Africa to be 'a magnificent cake', this had little to do with Africa's fountainhead position in humanity's history, or Africa's contributions to the origins of civilization; it had more to do with the desire to capture Africa's human and mineral wealth and use them for the benefit of the West.[14] To do this successfully, Europe needed to capture the African minds and re-programme Africans to think of themselves as Western men and women. The outcome was that the European colonial enterprise not only fractured the physical environment of Africa but extended to the appropriation of the African mind and a distortion of African cultural identities. With regard to this, Asante argues: '[W]e are either existing on our own "cultural" terms or the terms of others [...] [W]here will the African person find emotional and cultural satisfaction, if not in his/her own terms?'[15]

To add to the debates on history and culture, Gordon maintains that 'Africans like other human beings on earth are products of the environment. Geography is the handmaiden of history and culture. Thus, it can be concluded that all events of large significance take place within the setting of some culture.'[16] For this reason, the significance of culture lies in its being shared among people within the same territorial space to attain unity; it is not just for an individual's fulfilment; rather, it shapes the identity of the group of people and their destiny.

Mbakogu argues that cultural disintegration could be explained as the destabilization instituted when cultural changes go beyond the control of the people in the affected societies.[17] Under colonial expansion into Africa, African traditional cultures and values were seriously threatened. A key reason for cultural disintegration in Africa is the impact of the Berlin Conference, which in its division of Africa into 54 colonial territories, inserting borders in a few cases along natural features such as rivers, but more often with a ruler, paid little if any attention to the traditions, languages and values of the African people, with even less regard for them than for the continent's geography. The colonialists introduced their education systems, disrupting the ability of Africans to retain a memory of their past, and thus controlling their lives and subjugating them into slavery to serve white self-imposed masters.

---

14 Asante, *Facing South to Africa*, 115.
15 Asante, *Kemet, Afrocentricity, and Knowledge*, 8.
16 Gordon, "Towards an African Historiography," 28.
17 Mbakogu, "Is There Really a Relationship," 38.

These facts justify Gbotokuma's position that 'Africa has been weighed down by 400 years of exploitation, alienation, cultural and economic dismantlement, and the white man's recent deliberate political absolution of his conquest by renouncing colonialism, does not change anything'.[18] The main challenge facing Africans is to find solace in the reclamation of their history, culture and tradition to re-emerge from colonial brutalization, just as in the Akan culture of West Africa *sankofa* is used symbolically to represent the retrieval of memories in order to pave a path to the future. For this reason, the Afrocentric intellectual enterprise as led by Asante and the Afrocentric Temple Circle of scholars is framed by cosmological, epistemological, axiological and aesthetic issues.[19] Without reclaiming African history and culture, our decolonization efforts will remain a vain exercise.

Therefore, it is necessary for decolonization as a process of African reclamation to dismantle colonial culture by seeking first the restoration of the African mind from the wilderness of the Eurocentric intellectual heritage. If culture relates to attitudes, practices and a way of thinking about life in general, then it is true that colonialism has dismembered even the fabric of how Africans think about themselves. This is the essence of the damage caused, and it reduced Africans to non-beings. Therefore, cultural reclamation as a restorative process must aim to affirm the humanity of Africans and their way of life. Asante stresses that the only way for an African to find emotional and cultural satisfaction is when he/she is relocated to his/her own terms, meaning his/her own space or location.[20] Thus, the role of African culture is significant in shaping the cosmological, axiological and aesthetic issues as they relate to an African. According to Asante, they create a *djed* which helps Africans to be grounded in the traditions of their ancestors.[21]

Eurocentrism, Culture and Development in Africa

Eurocentrism is the cultural anchor of Euro-modernity. As I have highlighted in Chapter 3, Eurocentrism is described by Amin as one of the greatest ideological deformations of our time,[22] as it has arrogantly invented Europe as the centre of the world and claimed it to be the inventor of all positive human values. The colonial enterprise disrupted the progress

---

18 Zeke Gbotokuma, "Cultural Identity and Underdevelopment in Sub-Saharan Africa," *Voices from Africa* 4 (1996): 23.

19 Asante, *Kemet, Afrocentricity, and Knowledge*, 8.

20 Asante, *Kemet, Afrocentricity, and Knowledge*, 8.

21 Asante, *An Afrocentric Manifesto: Toward an African Renaissance*, 15.

22 Samir Amin, *Eurocentrism* (New York, NY: Monthly Review Press, 1989).

that Africa was making towards its own amalgamation and the attainment of a form of progress defined by African standards and experiences. Colonialism not only dismembered the physical environment of Africa but also disrupted African culture and converted Africans from the dignity of their own way of life into slavery and imposed on them a Western way of life.

Evidence abounds that the European writers distorted African history as part of their self-serving mission to negate Africa's cultural achievement. A key question is this: Can the European account of African history and culture be trusted, given that Europeans were persuaded by the colonial conquest mission in Africa? This European colonial mission was disguised behind the veil of civilization, salvation and development when it was their mission to rob Africa of its material resources and to disrupt Africans from their own way of life. Many of the European writers who set foot in Africa after the fifteenth century engaged in a study of the behaviour of Africans, their religion and tradition, but all too often with the intention of subjugating Africans and converting them into slaves (Onyenuru, 2014),[23] abroad or at home. They employed anthropological and historical methods in documenting their findings. It is fundamentally important to understand that the functional agenda of their anthropological study was not to understand Africans in good faith, aiming at building genuine relations rather than to conquer them. They could not see African history and culture as unique and valid, although they were different from their world view; rather, they rated their experiences and understanding as higher in a hierarchal order and placed those of Africans in a lower position.

In Mudimbe's view, the agenda of the colonialists was 'domination of physical space, reformation of native's minds and integration of their local economic histories into the Western perspectives'.[24] According to Mudimbe, the suppressive programme of the West, because of its colonial mission, produced two types of *ethnocentrism*.[25] The first is *epistemological ethnocentrism*, based on the perpetuated belief that nothing good can come from the Other, and even whatever it seems the Other knows is only a sign of participation in the universal, which is Western. Many Europeans to this day still believe that Africans have nothing intellectual to contribute to the international community other than learning and repeating what Europeans have taught them. Second, Mudimbe mentions what he refers to as *cultural ethnocentrism*.[26]

23 Valentin Y. Mudimbe, 2.

24 Valentin Y. Mudimbe, *The Invention of Africa: Gnosis, Philosophy and the Order of Knowledge* (Indianapolis, IN: Indiana University Press, 1988), 2.

25 Mudimbe, *The Invention of Africa*, 5.

26 Mudimbe, *The Invention of Africa*, 50.

This points to behavioural attitudes, beliefs and a general way of life rooted in the Western consciousness. Europeans believed that they were intellectually and culturally superior to the indigenous people they found in non-Western countries and that their redemption from their backward and barbarous way of life would be achieved by the injection of Western world views.

Colonial missionaries and anthropologists of the time misrepresented African history and culture as that of a downtrodden part of humanity, to reproduce their own imaginary 'African' culture, and cement their negative views about Africans. Wagner argues with reference to a colonially inspired mission that 'we might actually say that anthropologists invent the culture he believes himself to be studying, that the relation is more real for being his particular act and experiences than the things it relates'.[27]

In Onyenuru's (2014:5) opinion,[28] this paradigm of difference accounts for the normality, creative dynamism and achievements of the civilized world against the abnormality, deviance and primitiveness of what the Eurocentric view has labelled non-literate societies. Asante points out that

> the proponents of [a] western worldview have hedged their bets in a perspective that is moribund when it comes to looking at the outside world. Thus, they cannot truly grasp the significance of a revolutionary idea that would challenge the Eurocentric projection of its method as universal. However, the time has come for a total re-evaluation of both intellectual privilege and the assertion of European dominance in knowledge.[29]

It is because of this 'assertion of European dominance in knowledge' that when Europeans think of African development from their cultural ethnocentric perspective, they view it as a programme directed at 'upgrading' Africa to Europe's image, since Africa has for so long been projected as backward and populated by sub-human beings. The modern-day development project, which I have already shown to be traceable to the aftermath of World War II (after 1945) and Truman's Inaugural Speech in 1949,[30] has continued the assault on Africans' humanity by projecting Africans in the negative light of European and American glory. Truman, like many other European and North American

27 Roy Wagner, *The Invention of Culture* (Chicago, IL and London: University of Chicago Press, 1981), 27.

28 Okechukwu Onyenuru, Mudimbe on European Account of the African. Dominican Institute, Samanda, Ibadan, Nigeria, 2014, 5.

29 Asante, *African Pyramids of Knowledge*, viii.

30 Truman, *Point Four.*

writers, scholars and administrators, proceeded on the basis of premises that reveal their entrapment within narrow negative projections of Africa and Africans. He and his advisors did not see Africans as human beings with a history and culture and with the capabilities to uplift themselves to overcome their own development challenges. Rather, they objectify Africans into the status of children unable to help themselves to change their circumstances. For Ndlovu-Gatsheni,[31] 'the Truman version of development is deeply situated in the long history of the making of the modern world system and the invention of Africa that was accompanied by what Valentin Y. Mudimbe (1988) terms the "paradigm of difference"'.[32] This idea of development is a cultural hegemonic moment in which the 'superior' European logic and perspective cements its authority over those they consider backward, those whose humanity is doubted, except under the tutelage of Europeans.

For this reason, Eurocentric triumphalism inculcated a culture of despondency among Africans, leading them not to believe in their own capacity or that of their leaders to emerge beyond the imposed limitations. Thus, development became a project of assimilation and subjugation to spread the European cultural ethos. The idea that African notions of development were merely viewed in the context of an imitative process in which the non-Western subjects must regurgitate the experiences of the West was a further blow in the dislocation of the colonial subjects. For this reason, Escobar warns that 'the theory and practice of development is characterised by enormous errors in terms of cultural bias, misunderstandings and failed promises'.[33] For Olutayo, the implication of modernization is 'Europeanization'[34]; this implies that Europe is perceived as having the higher culture, which the lower culture of the underdeveloped nations by implication needs to develop. According to this premise, if the less-developed nations correctly implement the outlined imitative process, they will automatically reap the benefits of development enjoyed by 'high cultured' developed nations.

According to Brohman, modernization theory can be regarded, at best, as a heuristic device[35]; all along, it was too simplistic and too vague to be taken seriously as a comprehensive theory of development. In the end, it could

---

31 Ndlovu-Gatsheni, "The African Idea of Development," 4.

32 Mudimbe, *The Invention of Africa.*

33 Escobar, *Encountering Development,* 1995.

34 Akinpelu Olanrewaju Olutayo, "Gender, Society and Development," in *Nigerian Life and Culture: A Book of Readings,* eds. Olatunji Y. Oyeneye and Moses O. Shoremi (Ago-Iwoyi: Ogun State University, 1985), 190–208.

35 Brohman, "Universalism, Eurocentrism," 125.

not establish its relevance to the 'developing world', because it was really a celebration of the achievements of the 'advanced industrial countries'. Thus, the theory of modernization was a theory of violence that degraded the people located in the Global South, Africans in particular, in the quest to colonize and recolonize them. This theory literally undermined Africans as it labelled them backward people who needed civilization, when this ploy was a racist heuristic device. Brohman claims that the categories of 'modern' and 'traditional' employed by modernization theory are implausible because of their imprecision, narrowness and distance from reality.[36]

Brohman's claim directly corresponds with Dabaghian's summation in 1970 of 'acculturation', which refers to the process by which an individual goes from one culture to the next.[37] The process requires an individual to superimpose a second culture on top of the individual's first culture. In some ways, the colonized individual is still a member of the culture into which he/she is born, but in many ways, he/she has become a member of the culture in which he/she now lives (Onyenuru, 2014). Thus, blanket terms such as traditional and modern fail to do justice to the variability of societies both in the North and in the South, neither of which is homogeneous, and both of which are invariably fissured by factors such as class, gender, ethnicity and religion.[38]

The effects of this way of thinking have been disastrous in many ways to the lives of the non-Western societies. Thus, according to Asante, Eurocentric epistemology has produced in Africans a 'tortured consciousness', because 'one wanted to be something that one was not and the something that one wanted was perceived to be better than what one was'.[39] In the words of Du Bois, colonized people suffered from what he labelled 'double consciousness', which is the highest manifestation of alienation.[40] Such a people identify with the foreign base as the starting point towards the self, that is, from another self towards one's self, rather than the local being the starting point, which allows moving from the self to other selves.[41] This implies that the European development culture was not undertaken with good intentions regarding Africans; rather, it was a process of the destruction of a people's way of life, aimed at relocating them into another culture. For this reason, the challenge

36 Brohman, "Universalism, Eurocentrism," 125.

37 Jane Dabaghian, *Mirror of Man: Readings in Sociology and Literature* (Toronto: Little, Brown and Company, 1970).

38 Brohman, "Universalism, Eurocentrism."

39 Asante, *An Afrocentric Manifesto: Toward an African Renaissance*, 158.

40 Du Bois, *The Souls of Black Folk.*

41 Ngugi wa Thiong'o, *Globaletics: Theory and the Politics of Knowing* (New York, NY: Columbia University Press, 2012).

facing Africa is a reculturization grounded on African history and the lived experiences of African people, and to debunk European domination.

For most European neoclassical economists and related development theorists, the concept of economic growth is neither culture-specific nor based on historically changing conditions.[42] In the view of these theorists, economic growth is subject to its own laws, which they see as untouched by history and culture. Modernization views cultural factors such as ethnicity as nothing but obstacles to development that were rooted in backward societies, and which must be eradicated in order to usher in newness rooted in the Western way of thinking.

The newer neoliberal development thinking, like the older modernization approach, also employs universalist theoretical constructs based on unrealistic assumptions. This thinking still excludes much of the variability of non-Western society's social formations.[43] The post-war development thinking was dominated by an unrealistic and racist concept of modernization, which encouraged the construction of a single model of modernity, based on the experience of a few Western countries. However, if a change is to happen, in Africans' understanding of societal development, non-Western societies need to unlearn the European grand theories of development and recentre the debates within their own unique historical and cultural settings.

Prah raises the following fundamental questions with regard to development in the Global South:

> The question we (non-Western societies) face now is 'where are we headed?' How can we ensure that we get to where we wish to go? How do we get there? What sort of ideas and practices are needed to get us there? How can we use democratic theory and practice to achieve the goals of African emancipation and development?[44]

For this reason, Afrocentricity as a revolutionary paradigm seeks to challenge the way we think and conceptualize African development by re-centering Africans to their own culture as a base from which Africans must project their development trajectory. The notion of development, therefore, ought to be interrogated and deconstructed from an Afrocentric location, in order to unmask the hegemony and the thuggery of a Eurocentric bias. The African

---

42 Brohman, "Universalism, Eurocentrism."

43 Brohman, "Universalism, Eurocentrism."

44 Kwesi Kwaa Prah, *The Afrocentric Nation: The State of the Nation* (Cape Town: Centre for Advanced Studies of African Society, 2006).

development trajectory can only be relevant if Africans themselves claim their power to define what they want, guided by their own cultural and historical experiences. Without African-centredness as a guiding perspective, Africans will remain imitators of others' way of life, chained to the colonial agenda. Hence, Ndlovu-Gatsheni argues that

> [...] the reality about the African struggle for development is that it takes place within a modern world system that is resistant to decolonization and an international order that consistently works towards disciplining anti-systemic movements and forces so as to give the world system a new lease of life.[45]

The decolonization of the discourse of development, therefore, requires Africans to reassert and re-establish Africa as the centre of their own narratives. Asante argues that we cannot understand Africa's contribution to its own development and the world without examining the basis of its society.[46] Thus, African culture must be reclaimed and used as a resource and a base for interpreting and enriching African development debates, thus enabling Africans to map out their own path.

Afrocentricity, Culture and Development in Africa

In the second chapter of this study, Afrocentricity was unpacked as the guiding theory to challenge the idea of Western universality and the distortions it created in Africa's search for its identity and meaning of life. As I have pointed out, since the early fifteenth century, information about Africa has been falsified as a strategy to subdue Africans by placing them under the tutelage of European colonialists. Afrocentricity enters into debates on history and culture with the objective of recentring Africans within their own experiences to dispel deliberate distortions created to dismember the continent and its people. Moreover, it aims to denounce Eurocentric epistemology and its hegemonic stance as the foundation from which the people of Africa must interpret their realities.

Asante defines Afrocentricity as a consciousness, a quality of thought, mode of analysis and an actionable perspective where Africans seek, from agency, to claim a subject place within the context of African history and culture.[47] Therefore, Afrocentricity's main objective is cultural reclamation and the assertion of

---

45 Ndlovu-Gatsheni, "The African Idea of Development," 15.

46 Asante, *An Afrocentric Manifesto: Toward an African Renaissance*, 66.

47 Asante, *An Afrocentric Manifesto: Toward an African* Renaissance, 16.

the right of the African person to act as an agent in human history in an effort to unmask the illusion of being only on the fringes created by Eurocentrism. In her book, *The Afrocentric Paradigm*, Mazama explains that Afrocentricity is not merely a theory, but a *paradigm* that results in the reconceptualization of the social and historical reality of African people.[48]

Asante argues that 'it becomes absolutely necessary to accept the subject position of Africans within the context of their historical realities if progress is to be made in interpretation, analysis, synthesis, or construction'.[49] The primary contention in Afrocentricity is that the Eurocentric view has become an ethnocentric view, which elevates the European experience and downgrades all others.[50] Throughout the history of the last 2000 years, the major problem with European thought has been its 'inability to allow space for other cultures and therefore it becomes self-absorbed in some notion of Europe as the categorical universal for the world'.[51] Such authoritarianism has contributed to epistemic racism against non-European others, in particular Africans, who view their reality differently from the European canon of thought.

Afrocentricity enters the debate not as the absolute reverse of Eurocentrism, but as a particular perspective for analysis, one which does not seek to occupy all space and time as Eurocentrism has often done. By contrast, Karenga argues that Afrocentricity is about values and interests. He puts it this way: 'Afrocentricity is the quality of thought, practice and perspective that perceives Africans as subjects and agents of phenomena acting in their own cultural image and human interests'.[52] Monteiro-Ferreira affirms that

> [...] while Afrocentricity poses a severe criticism over the preponderant Eurocentric myths of universalism and challenges the colonizing concepts and racist theories that presides over the triumph of Western thought, it also offers the possibility of a non-hegemonic alternative perspective in the understanding of human expressions in our diverse multicultural society.[53]

Thus, the Afrocentrists argue for pluralism in philosophical views, without hierarchy. They advocate respect for all cultural centres with the specific

48 Mazama, *The Afrocentric Paradigm.*
49 Asante, *Facing South to Africa*, 1.
50 Asante, *An Afrocentric Manifesto: Toward an African Renaissance.*
51 Asante, *Facing South to Africa*, 3.
52 Karenga, *Introduction to Black Studies.*
53 Monteiro-Ferreira, *The Demise of the Inhumane*, 2.

aim of centring African experiences and history as a base from which *African* people must interpret their reality.

Since the 1980s, Afrocentricity has presented a revolutionary challenge to the ideology of white supremacy in education because of its insistence on centring African people, inside their own history, culture and science, rather than outside these subjects.[54] While colonial education was used as a tool for the *miseducation* of the African masses, according to Woodson,[55] Afrocentricity advocates that if education is to be relevant and substantive within African society, it must first address African historical and cultural experiences which have been deliberately ignored by Eurocentric scholars. Thus, this revolutionary approach in education begins by affirming the critical location of the researcher and the subject matter being researched. According to Asante, the critical location refers to the site where the researcher locates a researchable problem within a matrix of political, social and economic fields in order to determine the extent to which the problem is affected by internal and external forces.[56]

Unless the researcher is located in relation to the problem or phenomenon that is being studied, research loses meaningfulness and cannot bring about the change so greatly desired. Moreover, a dislocated approach to education contributes to a cultural dislocation of learners, as it takes them away from their own understanding of the world and makes them view reality from someone else's understanding. For authentic change to happen in terms of education, including Development Studies, Afrocentricity emphasizes *centricity*, which refers to a perspective that involves locating learners within the context of their own cultural references so that they can relate socially and psychologically to other cultural perspectives.[57] For this reason, Afrocentricity is particularistic in its approach to an understanding of phenomena and encourages every African person to become an agent in his/her own narrative, and not exist as a non-participative object of study.

Monteiro-Ferreira adds that Afrocentricity as a cultural theory is committed to the reclamation of ancient African classical civilization as the place for interpreting and understanding the history of African peoples, their narratives, myths, spirituality and cosmogonies.[58] The cultural reclamation is key in affirming the lost African ontological density as a result

---

54 Asante, *Facing South to Africa*, 48.

55 Carter G. Woodson, *The Miseducation of the Negro* (Washington, DC: Associated Press, 1933).

56 Asante, *Facing South to Africa*, 46.

57 Asante, *Facing South to Africa*.

58 Monteiro-Ferreira, *The Demise of the Inhumane*, 3.

of epistemological, psychological and physical violence Africans became subjected to.

Two types of multiculturalism are advanced here. The first is a particularistic multiculturalism, which has characterized the Western domination and racist culture. Its implications are that all non-Western societies must be subsumed under European culture in order for them to progress. The second is a non-hegemonic view of multiculturalism, which affirms the right for any human group to practise its own culture without being subjected to the dictates of another group. Afrocentricity seeks to advance the latter view and believes that unless respect is granted to all cultures, we will not attain the harmonious society that we desire.

Based on these reflections, it becomes necessary for Africans to relocate their lenses for a valid remapping of their development path in Africa and the African diasporas, grounded on their own cultural understanding. Afrocentricity calls for us systematically to displace European ways of thinking, being, feeling and so forth, and consciously replace them with ways that are germane to our own African cultural experiences.[59] Therefore, any idea of development rooted in mimicking others' experiences to the exclusion of the African experiences merely sustains the imperialist logic. For this reason, it is crucial to acknowledge that, Africa, with all of its natural resources, has been robbed for centuries, and that the robbery did not involve only organic and inorganic materials and minerals, but also a sense of place, knowledge and information.[60]

Africans need to be bold to embrace their own history and engage with the fact that their development did not begin with the arrival of Europeans on the African soil, but just like any other human beings everywhere in the world prior to colonialism, Africans could and did improve their own lives. Asante and Abarry in their book *African Intellectual Heritage: A Book of Sources* capture African works of imagination, invention, cultural dynamism, political engineering, religious and economic sophistication and originality as evidence of African creativity and innovation in surviving the challenges faced in diverse environments.[61] However, the colonial invasion ushered in a period of tribulations, which altered African ways of living and presented Africans as slaves who depended on their colonial masters for their survival. The project of development after World War II continued Western domination over non-Western societies and failed to bring the changes so greatly desired in those countries.

59 Mazama, "The Afrocentric Paradigm: Contours and Definitions," 388.

60 Asante, *Facing South to Africa*, 14.

61 Asante and Abarry, *African Intellectual Heritage*.

Ndlovu-Gatsheni[62] regards the Truman version of developmentalism as an offshoot of the colonialist enlightenment and modernity project, emanating from a complex and long history, mediated by the logics of coloniality, itself informed by domination, oppression and exploitation. Lushaba remarks:

> [T]he year 1950 does not mark the commencement of the continent's engagement with the question of development; rather it marked the beginning of new forms of imperialist domination, that is, neo-colonialism. As part of their strategy to maintain control over the continent, Western powers devised new forms of strategies to sustain their domination.[63]

Kwame Nkrumah, the first president of Ghana after independence in 1957, labelled these forms of control by the West as neocolonialism.[64] Thus, Lushaba notes that 1950 can only roughly be said to mark the beginning of the transition from the 'colonial' to the 'neocolonial mode' of production.[65] Therefore, development as we have come to know it remains a European interventionist project aimed at civilizing Africans into the European image. In view of this project, African people are deemed to be dependent beneficiaries who lack the capacity to change their own circumstances, hence Africans are not even considered to be capable agents for their own well-being.

The post-development theorists have been the most outspoken regarding their dissatisfaction with the concept and practice of 'development'. These theorists, most of whom originate from Western countries, Latin America and Asia, see development as a tool in the hands of the political elites of Western countries – a pattern for consolidating the Euro-North American hegemony.[66] Attempts at deconstructing the concept of development have been undertaken in order to reveal the operations of power and knowledge in development discourse and practices. Escobar, one of the leading voices in post-development theory, in his book *Encountering Development: The Making and Unmaking of the Third World*, describes development in the following manner:

> Development was – and continues to be for the most part – a top-down ethnocentric, and technocratic approach, which treats people

62 Ndlovu-Gatsheni, "The African Idea of Development," 4.

63 Lushaba, *Development as Modernity*, 2.

64 Nkrumah, *Neo-Colonialism*.

65 Lushaba, *Development as Modernity*.

66 Ewelina Róża Lubieniecka, *Does Post-Development Theory Find Alternatives to Westernization of International Relations? African Perspective*, 8th Pan-European Conference on International Relations (Poland: University of Warsaw, 2013), 2.

> and cultures as abstract concepts, statistical figures to be moved up and down in the charts of progress. Development was conceived not as a cultural process but instead a system of more or less universally applicable technical interventions intended to deliver some badly needed goods to a target population. It comes as no surprise that development became a force so destructive to the Third World cultures, ironically in the name of people's interests.[67]

Without a doubt, Escobar agrees that culture should be at the centre of our imaginations about development, as no society exists in a vacuum. Therefore, existing cultural patterns of the people must guide the direction of their own development, and not an externally imposed programme. Brohman points out that 'a complex factor such as culture could have no place in the neoclassical search for order in the "imperial development project" because it would expose the irrelevance of neoclassical economists and their idea of universal laws for economic growth'.[68] This implies that the liberation of Africa from neocolonial oppression lies in the reclamation of culture as a resource that must shape African development ideals. We need to factor in voices such as that of Julius Nyerere, the first president of Tanzania after independence, who opted to interpret development as the 'political mobilization of people for obtaining their own objectives' and not the objectives set by the others.[69]

Mbakogu notes that culture became increasingly important in the 1960s with the evident deficiencies regarding cultural diversity within modernization as a development model.[70] In response, in 1966, the United Nations Educational, Scientific, and Cultural Organization (UNESCO) General Conference, in Article 1 of its *Declaration*, stated that 'each culture has a dignity and value which must be respected and preserved' and that 'every people have the right and duty to develop its culture'.[71] In another UNESCO conference, namely the Intergovernmental Conference on the Administrative and Financial Aspects of Cultural Policies, held in 1970 in Venice, culture was emphasized as crucial for any policymaking agenda. The zenith of this conference was the message of Rene Maheu, the then UNESCO Director-General:

> Man is the means and the end of development; he is not the one-dimensional abstraction of homo economicus, but a living reality,

67 Escobar, *Encountering Development*, 44.
68 Brohman, "Universalism, Eurocentrism," 123.
69 Quoted in Lubieniecka, *Does Post-Development Theory Find Alternatives.*
70 Mbakogu, "Is There Really a Relationship," 40.
71 UNESCO, 1966, quoted in Mbakogu, "Is There Really a Relationship," 40.

> a human person. In the infinite variety of his needs, his potentials and his aspirations [...] in the concept of development the centre of gravity has thus shifted from the economic to the social, and we have reached a point where this shift begins to approach the cultural.[72]

Indeed, if Africans do not perceive development within their own cultural settings, they will remain shackled in oppression, in the shadow of the darker version of modernity as the only base from which to launch their development discourse. Hence, Afrocentricity espouses the cosmology, aesthetics, axiology and epistemology that characterize African culture.[73] Karenga identifies as the core cultural African characteristics the following: '[S]hared orientations, the centrality of the community, respect for tradition, a high level of spirituality and ethical concern, harmony with nature, the sociality of self-hood, veneration of ancestors and the unity of being'.[74] Thus, a development model that fails to observe the above elements continues to replicate a European cosmology and will not be able to give Africans a victorious consciousness.

Development cognizant of culture should thus not be conceived in an interventionist manner; rather, it should be seen as embracing people's way of life, which is their history, their attitudes, their traditions and their values, all of which enable them to give meaning to life. For this reason, this study argues that the development discourse can be greatly enriched by reframing it within an Afrocentric paradigm to enable African voices to take priority. Without this, Africa cannot experience a different future from the present situation. The challenge is for African scholars to transcend global colonial domination in the sphere of knowledge production and consider African culture as a resource to shape their thinking about development.

---

72 UNESCO, 1970, cited in Mbakogu, "Is There Really a Relationship," 40–41.

73 Mazama, "The Afrocentric Paradigm: Contours and Definitions," 393.

74 Karenga, *Introduction to Black Studies.*

Chapter 6

AFROCENTRICITY ON THE SIGNIFICANCE OF AFRICAN AGENCY IN DEVELOPMENT IN AFRICA

In Chapters 4 and 5, I discussed two prominent aspects of Afrocentricity, namely history and culture, and their significance for the reconceptualization of an Afrocentric development paradigm. Only European–North American history and culture informed the Truman development paradigm in the aftermath of World War II, as discussed in Chapter 3, and this model was a dismal failure in Africa because it was founded on erroneously universalized predictions grounded on modernization theory, which further deracinated Africans from their history and culture. This chapter discusses the role of African *agency* as the third aspect of Afrocentricity important for the reimagination of an Afrocentric development trajectory. The chapter examines Pan-Africanism and African nationalism as important ideological frameworks that undergird African agency to combat European domination. The chapter argues that the future of Africa can only be attained when Africans themselves act in their own best interests. Therefore, Africans must think, plan, implement and be the beneficiaries of their own development plans. They may not be reduced to puppets of the European games of conquest but should take charge of their own lives and map out their own futures.

It is important to note that the advent of modernity, which began in the late fifteenth century, ushered in European domination over Africa and dislocated Africans from their historical and cultural patterns of life, and converted Africans into European subjects. The domination of Africans from that time on set in motion the processes for Africa's dismemberment and loss of its own agency. As I have highlighted in Chapter 4, Africa was stripped of ownership of its contributions to world civilization and came to be considered a place occupied by sub-human savages without a history or culture. This was part of the European pattern of denigrating Africans to elevate the European human experience as the superior model for all. Thus, the invention of racism from the fifteenth century onwards became a strategy and a device to classify human beings in terms of their descriptive physical qualities and to create hierarchies, placing Africans in the lowest echelons of humanity. This racist claim was then used to justify the colonial invasion of Africa and the overthrow of African kings, making them and their people obedient subjects. It is for this reason that Asante argues that European domination has contributed to a denial of African agency since Africans were no longer allowed to govern themselves, but were treated as servants for colonial masters.[1]

Mazrui explains that European colonialism in Africa played havoc with African memory,[2] thus planting false memories, amnesia and nostalgia through the colonial education system. The European colonial mission dismembered the *physical* environment of Africa to extract mineral resources for use by Europe as planned during the Berlin Conference of 1884/85. It also negatively affected the psychological dimension of African people. To paint colonization as a noble undertaking to salve Europeans' conscience and colour their perceptions, the colonial endeavour required justification. This included the appropriation of the African people's bodies and minds, turning them into European subjects through a Eurocentric education system.[3]

Similarly, the modernization theory of the 1950s, which represented a continuation of the European supremacist civilizational and enlightenment movement, depicted non-Western societies, Africa in particular, as backward and prehistoric. The only means by which these societies could be developed, according to the Europeans and North Americans, was through a forceful injection of Western values and culture.[4] Thus, from the parochial European perspective, Africa had not achieved any development on its own, and it allegedly remained stagnant because of primitive cultural traditions. European scholars portrayed Africa as a continent of despotic civilizations with no legacy of the kinds of democratic principles that are enshrined in the West's self-image.

According to Mazama, there are about four key assumptions that inform Eurocentric ideological framework, which plays a foremost and negative role as far as African people are concerned.[5] First, it is assumed that all human

---

1 Asante, *An Afrocentric Manifesto: Toward an African Renaissance.*

2 Ali A. Mazrui, "The Re-invention of Africa: Edward Said, V. Y. Mudimbe, and Beyond," *Research in African Literatures* 3, no. 36 (2005): 77.

3 Lehasa R. Moloi, "An Afrocentric Development Paradigm: A Model that Matters for Africa," in *Reinventions and Contestations of Thought-power: Emerging Perspectives on Pan-Africanism,* eds. Percy-Sledge Chigora, Richard R. Mahomva, and Majahana Lunga (Harare: LAN Readers, 2018), 120–35.

4 Lerner, *The Passing of Traditional Society.*

5 Mazama, Ama, *Afrocentricity and the Critical Question of African Agency,* 2014, 1.

beings evolve along the same linear pattern. Second, it is tacitly assumed that the European experience is universal. Third, Europeans are assumed to be superior. Fourth, 'others' are defined and judged according to European supremacist standards. This implies that the essence of the European ideological framework rests, among other things, on a flawed belief in the superiority and universality of the European experience to the exclusion of others.

Afrocentricity as an emerging contrasting and combative paradigm against European domination seeks to confirm the centrality of Africans within their own historical and cultural experiences, and it emphasizes the significance of Africans becoming their own agents in pursuit of their own future. This paradigm stresses that Africa before the arrival of Europeans had its own complex civilizations, including the kind that Europeans regard as valid and important – civilizations that produce great kings, impressive empires and elaborate technological skills.[6,7]

Here I advance an argument that there is no African future unless Africans themselves retell their own tales and reframe their projections of what their future entails within the frames of their own history, culture and agency. For this reason, any serious development agenda aimed at contributing to African resurgence must be informed by African agencies, which must enable Africans to think from where they stand. Asante maintains that we Africans 'are not yet free when in the imagination of some of our young people we are still hoping to discover that Africa is not in our past'.[8] Therefore, an African development discourse needs to be sensitive to cultural dynamics and history and must be contextualized to include African axiology, aesthetics, cosmology and epistemology. African development processes can only be seen as relevant if they are initiated as endogenous processes that affirm African people's wishes and are driven by them as subjects and not objects of European development agendas (such as that expressed in the post–World War II development paradigm).

Defining the Concept of African Agency

According to Asante, 'an agent means a human being who is capable of acting independently in his or her own best interest'.[9] Agency refers to the ability to provide the psychological and cultural resources necessary to advance human freedom. The long history of European domination over Africa that began

6 Asante and Abarry, *African Intellectual Heritage.*
7 Mazrui, "The Re-invention of Africa," 77.
8 Asante, *Facing South to Africa*, ix.
9 Asante, *An Afrocentric Manifesto: Toward an African Renaissance*, 40.

in the fifteenth century rendered Africans as incapable people and it contributed to the weakening of African agency. Within the context of Afrocentricity as a paradigm of African Renaissance, the key challenge is the restoration of African people within their history and culture to enable them to become their own agents in the interpretation of their own lived experiences. Asante further argues that 'when agency does not exist or is disempowered, we have the condition of marginality, and the worst form of marginality is to be marginal within your own story'.[10] Thus, white racial domination implies more than marginalization: it also means the obliteration of the presence, meaning, activities, or the image of the African people.[11] Colonial domination has resulted in a loss of African ontological density, relegating Africans to the periphery of the European experience.

According to Mazama, because of colonial domination, as 'Africans became dislocated, and lost sight of themselves in the midst of European decadence and madness, it became increasingly difficult for them to orient their lives in a positive and constructive manner'.[12] Due to lack of proper African informed political consciousness, our agency continues to be grounded on un-African grounds, on foreign ones. It is directed towards self-annihilation as we were made, as a result of colonization, to by-pass ourselves as we speak and act to serve the interests of others, yet to inaugurate our own downfall. For this reason, the restoration of active African agency demands that Africans must be able to find a strong place to stand, which is their own intellectual and cultural position. Africans must therefore relocate to their own cultural and historical terms as a standpoint from which they can engage with the world as free agents.[13] The re-development of African societies requires Africans to take charge of their own lives, shaking off domination, and map out their own development path within the ideal of Pan-Africanism. Asante warns:

> Africans cannot enter their imaginary future on the wagons of victimhood, hounded by the dogs of marginality, with their minds centered only on their colonial past. The idea of African development future not informed by African history, culture and agency only serves to sustain the perpetuity of the colonial culture of domination and African marginalization.[14]

---

10 Asante, *An Afrocentric Manifesto: Toward an African Renaissance*, 41.

11 Asante, *An Afrocentric Manifesto: Toward an African Renaissance.*

12 Mazama, "The Afrocentric Paradigm: Contours and Definitions," 388.

13 Asante, *An Afrocentric Manifesto: Toward an African Renaissance*, 15.

14 Molefi Kete Asante, *Afrocentricity's Afrofuturism and the Countdown to the Future.* Conference paper delivered in Berlin, Germany, November 2–4 (2018), 10.

The modern-world system of European colonial domination has trodden down the humanity of African people and their rights to existence, distorted their history and labelled them sub-humans and savage and incapable of innovation. Mazama, therefore, maintains that the challenge facing Africans is monumental because it rests on their ability to systematically displace European ways of thinking, being, feeling and so forth and consciously replace them with ways that are germane to their own African cultural experience.[15] The imposition of Europe under the guise of objectivity and universalism is part of a narrative of white superiority, a racial mythology, based on the rather strange belief on the parts of whites that they are superior to Africans, allegedly giving them a right to establish and maintain a hierarchy over blacks by force of arms or customs or laws or habits.[16] The moral aesthetics of Afrocentricity as a paradigm advancing African renaissance is then to resituate Africans in the centre of African narratives of place, time and space. Thus, Afrocentricity demonstrates that the dislocation of Africans from the centre of their own history is a form of intellectual and cultural terrorism, constantly attacking Africans' concept of self and idea of time.[17]

Since the end of World War II, Africans and other ex-colonized peoples have increasingly demanded that development be made one of the important human rights, the right to development. Historically, the Bandung Conference of 1955 was the turning point. Ndlovu-Gatsheni believes that the spirit of decolonization, South–South solidarity and a principle of non-alignment informed this conference.[18] The conference laid the foundation for the struggle to decolonize and democratize international society to attain equitable representation in global decision-making bodies. It, therefore, called for a New International Economic Order (NIEO). For Ndlovu-Gatsheni, this made sense in a global terrain in which it was known that a combination of enslavement, colonization, apartheid and neocolonialism actively denied development to those regions of the world that experienced colonial difference.[19] While the conference was a great initiative in the spirit of collaboration among ex-colonized nations, the critical thing for Africa was to find its own voice, rooted in the vision of Pan-Africanism and African nationalism.

The development future of Africa means that Africans themselves must not exist as mere dependent beneficiaries of exogenous development projects and programmes. The call has increasingly been for Africans to become active

15 Mazama, "The Afrocentric Paradigm: Contours and Definitions," 388.

16 Asante, *An Afrocentric Manifesto: Toward an African Renaissance*, 136.

17 Asante, *Facing South to Africa*.

18 Ndlovu-Gatsheni, "The African Idea of Development," 5.

19 Ndlovu-Gatsheni, "The African Idea of Development," 3.

participants in the ideation, planning and implementation of their dreams. It is, after all, impossible to think of the future of Africa if Africans themselves no longer exist. African agency, therefore, denotes active participation by people of African descent in all spheres of life, be it political, social, economic or cultural – they must be active in asserting their presence and taking charge to define their own future(s). In relation to development, active agency thus implies that Africans must resist European thinking and replace it with their own strategies for success. In this regard, Ndlovu-Gatsheni[20] points out that African development, in the words of Marcus Garvey, means 'a constant and consistent African search for self-improvement'. It is also defined by Julius Nyerere to mean 'political mobilization of people for attaining their own objectives' and not the objectives set by others (quoted in Estera, 1996:7). Although it is important for Africa to create collaborative interventions within the bigger Global South, the main call is for Africans themselves to rely on their own cultural traditions as a base from which to engage the world.

The main problem with development theory to date is its deliberate omission of African voices in shaping development discourse. This is a major cause of the paternalistic tendencies that have projected European ideas as superior to others. Ndlovu-Gatsheni argues that Development Studies in Africa has remained deeply intercalated within the Euro-American modernist and civilizing mission.[21] Thus, development remains a heuristic device used in the domination of Africans; as a product of global imperial designs, it serves the agenda of maintaining imbalances in decision-making, thus chaining Africans to preconceived ideologies without any hope of escaping. Therefore, African victory against epistemic and physical domination by Europe requires Africans to take charge by first relocating to their own terms of reference; this means shifting the location of reasoning from Europe to Africa. This would enable Africans to interrogate all concepts rooted in a European cultural ethos, such as democracy, development, progress and the nation-state, which have been projected as that which the continent needs in order to advance.

Mazama emphasizes that 'a people's worldview determines what constitutes a problem for them and how they solve problems'.[22] Afrocentricity demands that the scholars of Africa reflect on the ontology, cosmology, axiology and aesthetics of African people and that they be centred in their own experiences to step away from domination by others.

---

20 Ndlovu-Gatsheni, "The African Idea of Development," 1.

21 Ndlovu-Gatsheni, *Coloniality of Power*, 48.

22 Mazama, "The Afrocentric Paradigm: Contours and Definitions," 399.

Problematic Agency and African Development Impasse

In Chapter 3, I discussed the epistemological crisis affecting the conception of development as an ideology and a field of study and practice in Africa. I showed that the discourse of development is still embedded in the discourse and effects of the Euro-North American mission to maintain that region's hold over the Global South, and Africa in particular, so that claims of development by those who offer it to Africans as the objects of development are disingenuous. If genuine development is desired, we need to acknowledge that the post–World War II development vision outlined through the Point Four programme of Harry Truman in 1949 is demonstrably irrelevant to the advancement of the African continent (if it ever was relevant) and cannot be effective. Ndlovu-Gatsheni has shown that this version of development cannot be divorced from its complex and long history, mediated by the logics of coloniality, resulting in the oppression and exploitation of non-Western countries in general, and Africa in particular.[23] This idea of development was informed by the historical experiences of a few Western countries and their culture and was driven by their own agents.

Euro-North American agents in the form of development experts, administrators, including academics such as historians, sociologists and anthropologists, facilitated the European colonial conquest mission, disguised as an emancipatory endeavour. For this reason, they could not act as African agents serving the best interests of the African continent and its people. To this effect, the European-conceptualized notion of development, although it was relevant for Europeans, is a straitjacket when it is imposed ostensibly to guide an African development trajectory.

According to Adedeji, the paradigm of development guided by Truman's interventionist development propaganda was backed by what Adedeji terms the development merchant system, which is in turn driven by the Bretton Woods Institutions as the agents that finance the implementation of this exogenous development agenda.[24] Therien claims that the development management system exists as a consortium comprised of the International Monetary Fund (IMF), the World Bank, the World Trade Organization, various international non-governmental organizations and multinational corporations.[25] These agents have long worked together to advance the Bretton Woods paradigm of development as part of the continuation of the hegemonic Truman version of developmentalism.

23 Ndlovu-Gatsheni, "The African Idea of Development."

24 Adedeji, *From the Lagos Plan of Action*, 4.

25 Therien, "Beyond the North-South Divide."

'The neoliberal ideas that underpinned these organizations included the broad endorsement of the project of globalization, giving corporate business a prominent role in both policymaking and in proposed models of development governance and growth, believing that the institutions of global governance themselves are the key creative actors in the facilitation of development and growth'. This collection of ideas has sometimes been labelled 'the Washington Consensus'.[26] Therefore, it is highly unlikely that such institutions would act as agents advancing African development interests since they are inclined towards serving the neocolonial agenda of Western nations.

In sum then, as P. W. Preston[27] also suggests, development thinking since the mid-1940s has been based on three main pillars: economic growth, state planning and international aid. This idea of development has precipitated and then perpetuated the neocolonial capture of African states even in the post-independence era to sustain Western domination. Suffice it to conclude that the idea of European development has been driven by European knowledge, historical experiences, culture and agency, and was, and is, not designed to serve African interests. As a result, African states remain located at the lowest level of the capitalist global structures and continue to be used as a source of raw materials and cheap labour to support the exogenous colonial agenda of the Western nations.

As Ndlovu-Gatsheni has shown, the long-term consequences of the Berlin Scramble in 1884–1885 was the submerging of the African people within the territorial boundaries created by Europeans.[28] This has destabilized Africa's traditional governance systems and rendered Africans ineffective agents in their defence against colonial brutality. African kingdoms were replaced with the foreign notion of the modern nation-state, based on a European ethos and facilitating European business interests in the wake of the Berlin Scramble. Ndlovu-Gatsheni argues that the construct of the modern nation-state applied to Africa at the Berlin Conference can be traced back much further, to the year 1648, when the Treaty of Westphalia was signed at the end of the Thirty Years War (1618–1648) in Europe.[29] The Westphalian Peace Treaty signalled the institutionalization and norming of a modern world order

---

26 Lance Taylor, "Editorial: The Revival of the Liberal Creed – The IMF and the World Bank in a Globalized Economy," *World Development* 25, no. 2 (1997): 145–52.

27 Cited in Bjorn Hettne, *Development Theory and the Three Worlds: Towards an International Political Economy of Development* (2nd Ed.) (Harlow and New York, NY: Longman, 1995), 36.

28 Ndlovu-Gatsheni, "The Entrapment of Africa," 339.

29 Ndlovu-Gatsheni, "The Entrapment of Africa," 337.

as a juridical political formation.[30] While the European states recognized each other's sovereignty, they did not recognize non-European people's sovereignty. The Berlin Scramble was a further manifestation of the European disregard for the humanity of non-Europeans, in this case, particularly of African people and their political formations. Therefore, even in the post-independence era, the political attempts of African leaders to exercise their political agency had to be made within colonially created boundaries. The post-independence nation states were, therefore, the direct products of the Berlin Conference's mapping of African territory; they were not designed by Africans for Africans but were imposed within the logic of a colonial paradigm of difference.

Afrocentricity, Agency and Development in Africa

In Chapter 2, I discussed Afrocentricity at length as a perspective on existence that privileges African agency within the context of African history and culture, transcontinentally and trans-generationally. In the words of Mazama, in 'the past two decades Afrocentricity became a formidable pan-African ideology that introduced fundamental changes in the way African people interpret their reality'.[31] Its ability to theorize and articulate the disturbing conditions of African people is the main reason for its appeal intellectually. Moreover, the remedy that Afrocentricity suggests, which is centralizing African realities and calling for Africans to relocate to their own centre helps in building an African victorious consciousness as a mechanism to overthrow domination. According to Monteiro-Ferreira,

> Afrocentricity remained an alternative paradigm autonomous from ethnocentric Eurocentrism, and as a truly liberating framework for the recognition of the African philosophical and scientific contribution to civilization, and an approach to re-centering on an African ethics of human existence that is self-determined and self-defined. [...] there is no liberation for a materially and mentally colonized people of Africa unless they will be able to exist outside the prison box of the European paradigm. Afrocentricity as a theory advancing the significance of African agency in all matters affecting an African life recuperates the classical African historical past and the Kemetic philosophical thought as the fundamental sites of African liberation.[32]

---

30 Michael Hardt and Antonio Negri, *Empire* (Cambridge, MA: Harvard University Press, 2000).

31 Mazama, "The Afrocentric Paradigm: Contours and Definitions," 387.

32 Monteiro-Ferreira, *The Demise of the Inhumane*, 89.

It offers the methodological and epistemological potential to embrace the ontological, cosmological and functional aspects of African life and experience as a means to overcoming European domination.

Thus, if Africans do not relocate to their own terms of reference, as is suggested by Afrocentricity, they will remain trapped in an epistemological prison that thwarts their own understanding of the world, and will have nothing to contribute to the world, being trapped in a dehumanizing acceptance of the darker version of modernity. The fundamental call made by Afrocentric scholars is the need for an epistemological reclamation grounded on the lived experiences of the African people, which paves a path for their re-emergence against almost more than 500 years of European domination.[33,34] Mazama reminds us that

> one of the consequences of the denial of African agency has been the conspicuous absence of African people in the narration of history. Their presence became invisibilised even to themselves since their existence was denied; thus, Africans have been negated in the system that privileges white racial domination.[35]

For Monteiro-Ferreira, the colonial and imperialist powers, European and American, and their extensions on the African continent are dependent on the system of racism and can only be overridden through structural changes whose source has to be identified with African material, spiritual and cosmological realities.[36] Omari also concedes that it is only through an Afrocentric cosmological reclamation that the free agency and worth of African people in their own business will be restored, as it pertains to the African traditional values of harmony, justice, equality and diligence.[37] Along similar lines, Article 4 of *Agenda 2063*, published by the African Union Commission, presents the following vision: 'We rededicate ourselves to the enduring Pan African vision of an integrated, prosperous and peaceful Africa, driven by its 'own citizens' and representing a dynamic force in the international arena'.[38]

---

33 Asante, *An Afrocentric Manifesto: Toward an African Renaissance.*

34 Mazama, *The Afrocentric Paradigm.*

35 Mazama, *Afrocentricity and the Critical Question*, 9.

36 Monteiro-Ferreira, *The Demise of the Inhumane*, 71.

37 Omari, T. Peter, *Kwame Nkrumah: The Anatomy of an African Dictatorship* (New York, NY: Africana Publishing Corporation, 1970), 193.

38 African Union, *Agenda 2063: The Africa We Want* (Addis Ababa: African Union Commission, 2015), 1.

This affirms the view expressed by Afrocentricity that 'unless Africans themselves become their own agents in outlining the vision of development and participate in its implementation they will remain entrapped within the prison box of colonial domination'.[39] This construct adjustment will lead Africans to the renaissance that is necessary in Africa, and thus in African Studies, and will assist in Africa's own achievement of a political, cultural, economic and social renaissance.

In the following two subsections, I examine two ideological frameworks that have guided and framed the expression of African agency to challenge European domination over Africans, namely Pan-Africanism and African nationalism.

Pan-Africanism

According to Asante, Pan-Africanism grounded on Afrocentricity is the best defence of African people and their resources, and it is an expression of a much-needed agency to overthrow the European–North American hegemony.[40] Asante believes that the Pan-African Congresses, which began in the nineteenth century, were meant to establish the framework for African unity. Asante's definition of Afrocentricity,[41] therefore, includes the fact that it is a Pan-African intellectual perspective that privileges African agency within the context of African history and culture transcontinentally and trans-generationally. Therefore, Afrocentricity, although it was conceptualized by Asante in America, does not apply only to African Americans in the African diaspora. Rather, its vision and mission extend to continental Africans and the world at large for the advancement of African liberation. Afrocentricity as a pan-African ideology and intellectual *djed* believes that the authentic call for Pan-African unity must be grounded on an understanding of African history, culture and Africans as their own agents of change, and it must be informed by African epistemology. Therefore, Pan-Africanism literally connotes an *all-African* movement that embraces the ideology of liberation for continental and diasporic Africans in every political, economic and cultural sphere.[42]

---

39 Asante, *An Afrocentric Manifesto: Toward an African Renaissance*, 66.

40 Asante, *Facing South to Africa*, 95.

41 Asante, *An Afrocentric Manifesto: Toward an African Renaissance*, 2.

42 Ghelawdewos Araia, *The Historical and Ideological Foundations of Pan-Africanism*, Institute of Development and Education for Africa, 2014. http://www.africanidea.org/pan-Africanism.html, 1.

According to Legum, the Pan-African ideology and movement began not in the homeland of Africa[43] but in the diaspora – to be specific in the Caribbean and the United States of America. At the base of the formation of this movement lies deep feelings of dispossession, oppression, persecution and rejection suffered by African people worldwide. It was through the Pan-African Congresses that Africans from the rest of the world spoke the truth directly to the colonial powers and revealed the hypocrisies, conceits and double standards within the modern world system and global orders. The Pan-African Congresses' initiatives became an avenue to make an appeal to the nations of the world 'to protect the Africans from depredations of the European empire builders'.[44]

Several great historical incidents fuelled the Pan-African movement. The first was the Haitian Revolution, first led by Boukman in 1791 and later by Toussaint Louverture. It culminated in the founding of the first Black Republic in the Western hemisphere in 1804.[45,46] Another great historical event that raised the political consciousness and confidence of Africans on the continent and in the diaspora, and that added fuel to Pan-Africanism, was the resounding victory of Ethiopia over Italy in the battle of Adwa in 1896.[47,48] Repatriation became a manifestation of early Pan-Africanism in the last quarter of the seventeenth century and the first decade of the nineteenth century, but race relations became another dimension to propel Pan-African resistance.

In 1897, W. E. B. Du Bois started to talk about the need for a pan-Negro movement.[49] The first Pan-African Congress was held in London in 1900, led and sponsored by the Trinidadian barrister Henry Sylvester Williams, who is credited with coining the concept of Pan-Africanism.[50] Du Bois became a part of this conference. It was during this congress that Du Bois spoke his famous prophetic lines: 'The problem of the twentieth century is the problem of the colour line – the relations of the darker to the lighter races of men in Asia and Africa, in America and the islands of the sea.'[51] Although there were many important figures in the early stages of the growth

43 Colin Legum, *Pan-Africanism: A Short Political Guide* (New York, NY: Frederick A. Praeger, 1965), 14.

44 George Padmore, *Pan-Africanism or Communism* (New York, NY: Double-Day Anchor, 1972), 96.

45 Araia, *The Historical and Ideological Foundations of Pan-Africanism*, 2.

46 Ndlovu-Gatsheni, "The Entrapment of Africa," 340.

47 Araia, *The Historical and Ideological Foundations of Pan-Africanism*.

48 Legum, *Pan-Africanism*.

49 Legum, *Pan-Africanism*, 24.

50 Legum, *Pan-Africanism*.

51 Quoted in Legum, *Pan-Africanism*, 25.

of Pan-African ideas, the two most dominant political figures became W. E. B. Du Bois and Marcus Garvey.[52,53] Asante maintains that the Pan-Africanists during the first conference put their hands together in the *harambee* spirit to demand the liberation of Africans from colonial oppression.[54]

The third Pan-African Congress was held in London and Brussels in 1921, followed by the fourth, which also held sessions in London and Lisbon in 1923.[55] The fifth Pan-African Congress, the last of the series of congresses directly led by Du Bois, was held in New York in 1927. The sixth Pan-African Congress was held in 1945 in Manchester in Britain, and it brought together Pan-Africanists from the diaspora and Africa. The Africans who attended include Kwame Nkrumah from Ghana, Jomo Kenyatta from Kenya, Wallace Johnson from Sierra Leone, Peter Abrahams from South Africa and Marko Hlubi, representing the African National Congress.[56]

Three significant aspects of Pan-Africanism could be identified throughout these meetings: Pan-Africanism as an avenue for waging the anti-colonial struggle; Pan-Africanism as a protest against Euro-American racism against black people in the diaspora and on the African continent; and Pan-Africanism as a quest for African unity.[57] Legum explains that the Pan-African political movement came home to the African continent in 1958 under the leadership of Kwame Nkrumah, but that its cultural wing remained in the diaspora.[58]

The All-Africa People's Conference of 1958 became the precursor to the establishment of the Organization of African Unity in 1963, which in turn became a precursor for the African Union in 2002. Therefore, the Organization of African Unity and later the African Union remain critical vehicles in advancing African agency within the continent to oppose European domination. Although it needs to be noted that the journey has not been easy, these structures remain critical in providing an avenue for African voices to be heard. However, according to Ndlovu-Gatsheni, Pan-Africanism as an expression of African agency paradoxically continues to be in conflict with African nationalism, as some Africans remain reluctant to sacrifice territorial nationalism for the greater goal of Pan-African unity.[59] Nkrumah coined the

---

52 Araia, *The Historical and Ideological Foundations of Pan-Africanism.*

53 Legum, *Pan-Africanism.*

54 Asante, *Facing South to Africa*, 95.

55 Legum, *Pan-Africanism.*

56 Legum, *Pan-Africanism*, 31–32.

57 P. Olisanwuche Esedebe, *Pan-Africanism: The Idea and the Movement, 1776–1963.* (Washington, DC: Howard University Press, 1970).

58 Legum, *Pan-Africanism*, 38.

59 Ndlovu-Gatsheni, "The Entrapment of Africa," 341.

slogan of seeking a political kingdom as the first step in decolonization, and by 1965 already articulated the problem of 'neocolonialism', which makes it difficult for African leaders to translate their hard-won political decolonization into a desperately needed economic decolonization.[60] Nkrumah published *Africa Must Unite* in 1963 when he realized the key problems with attaining the ideal of a political kingdom.[61]

The main challenge that faces African leaders is how to forge a pan-ethnic national unity to overcome the possibility of internal fragmentation of the newly independent states. This challenge has been expressed through nation-building and state-making processes. According to Nkrumah, the greatest danger facing Africa is neocolonialism, and its major instrument, balkanization.[62] Balkanization describes the breaking up of Africa into small and weak states, which makes it difficult to sustain continental and nation-state unity. For this reason, Asante's Afrocentricity argues that the quest for Pan-Africanism must not be merely symbolic but must also be deepened within the philosophical soil of African culture as a resource (Asante, 2018). To be specific, Asante argues that the 'classical past must be viewed as a resource for an African renaissance'.[63] Asante emphasizes that 'the new revolutionary moment in which African people interrogate and locate within their own history the values, concepts, and ideals that are essential for a reinvigorated society can be advanced by seriously engaging the Nile Valley civilizations'. Without this, there can be no authentic African Renaissance, nor any useful future for Africa.

African nationalism

African nationalism, like Pan-Africanism, became an ideological framework used by African leaders to express their own agency to rebuild dismembered African communities after independence. While African nationalism was a necessary call, it remains important to scrutinize the impact of coloniality in the conceptions of these concepts letting us use them without careful attention to how they have been hijacked by modern discourses. Just as Mazama warns us that 'our failure to recognize the roots of such ideas in the European cultural ethos has led us, willingly or unwillingly, to agree to footnote status in the white man's book'.[64] Epistemological colonization of

60 Nkrumah, *Neo-Colonialism.*

61 Kwame Nkrumah, *Africa Must Unite* (London: PANAF, 1963).

62 Nkrumah, *Africa Must Unite,* 173.

63 Asante, *An Afrocentric Manifesto: Toward an African Renaissance,* 67.

64 Mazama, "The Afrocentric Paradigm: Contours and Definitions," 387.

political terms under modernity also meant that African leaders in the post-independence era fell into the trap of legitimizing European-created borders in Africa. Asante affirms this point by stating that

> [...][t]he boundaries of nation-states established by Europe are unstable and serve to exacerbate inadequate communication, ethnocentric worldviews, poor interstate transportation, marginal trade with neighbours, lack of crop diversity, overemphasis on export crops to maintain connection to former colonial powers, and lack of regional planning authorities.[65]

Nationalism can be defined as an ideological movement, for the attainment of self-government and independence on behalf of a group, with the aim of becoming a nation.[66] For this reason, Breuilly defines nationalism *as a political movement seeking to exercise state power and justifying such action with nationalist arguments*,[67] which are the existence of a nation, the importance of the interest of this nation, or that the nation must be independent with the attainment of political sovereignty. According to Gunn, the concept of nationalism flourished in Europe, especially Western Europe, particularly during the nineteenth century, when sovereign states developed very strong feelings about nationality.[68] Ndlovu-Gatsheni argues that 'a balanced assessment of the character of African nationalism is to depict it as both a derivative discourse as well as a new creation of the African people as they responded to colonialism'.[69] Along similar lines, Chatterjee[70] suggests that 'while nationalism in Africa has been significant in the re-organization of African societies to resist colonialism, it remains a 'plagiaristic discourse' that was entangled with colonialism'.

Africans have had three options in their pursuit of nationalistic discourse: 'reproducing pre-colonial nationalistic formations; embracing existing colonial states; or re-creating a new pan-African political formation'.[71] On the whole,

---

65 Asante, *Facing South to Africa*, 86.

66 Anthony Douglas Smith, *Theories of Nationalism* (London: Gerald Duckworth, 1971).

67 John Breuilly, *Nationalism and the State* (Manchester: Manchester University Press, 1993), 2.

68 Jean Philippe Gunn, "African Nationalism from the Colonial Period to the Post-Colonial Period," *Social Sciences Studies Journal* 4, no. 20 (2018): 2989.

69 Ndlovu-Gatsheni, "The Entrapment of Africa," 342.

70 Partha Chatterjee, *Nationalist Thought and the Colonial World: A Derivative Discourse?* (London: Zed Books, 1986), cited in Ndlovu-Gatsheni, "The Entrapment of Africa," 341.

71 Ndlovu-Gatsheni, Sabelo J. "The Entrapment of Africa," 342.

African leaders in the post-independence era settled for the production of postcolonial nation-states grounded on the modernist paradigm.

African conceptions of nationalism could not escape the immanent logic of colonialism, as they were shaped by the colonizers' models. Hence, newly appointed or elected African leaders legitimized the colonial borders that were created by the imperialists and failed to reconstitute Africa from their own newly designed framework: African agency remained trapped in the very paradigm these leaders were seeking to overthrow. When Asante, therefore, published *Afrocentricity: The Theory of Social Change*,[72] his intention was to give African people the sense that we are capable and that we have our own agency to operate in our own best interests. For the Pan-African vision to become a reality, African leaders must express their willingness and have the courage to work with their citizens to remap African borders in ways that can best serve their interests.

According to Smith,[73] colonialism brought modernization to Africa, but it also destroyed traditional structures and established a new type of social class constituted by the intelligentsia, a bourgeoisie and a small working class who are an interest group, and the members have in common a finance and an economic system similar to that in the colonial period. What was at play was the manifestation of a colonized imagination and a constrained agency. This leads to the conclusion that, although Africans have deployed Pan-Africanism and African nationalism as strategies to express their own agency in the fight against European domination, such an agency remains entrapped in the logic of imperialization. African decolonization efforts must, therefore, be deepened to deal with the profound cultural, psychological and epistemological dimensions of colonialism to overthrow European domination. For this reason, Afrocentricity encourages Africans to

> step outside of the European thinking frames and its models and interpretation of reality to generate new acquisition of knowledge. Afrocentricity challenges the orientation to history foreign to the history of the African subject; it demands an epistemological location that places an African inside the African experience framed by African codes, symbols, motifs, myths that creates an African sense of being in the world arena.[74]

72 Asante, *Afrocentricity: The Theory of Social Change.*
73 Smith, *Theories of Nationalism*, 74.
74 Monteiro-Ferreira, *The Demise of the Inhumane*, 2.

Thus, Pan-Africanism and African nationalism, as far as the argument in this book is concerned, must be rooted within Afrocentricity as a paradigm and must seek to reclaim the centricity of Africans in the narrative of their own lives, not to live as the surrogates of a European cultural ethos. It is important, as Asante has suggested, to ensure that 'their agency is framed within the African cosmological, epistemological, axiological and aesthetic issues'.[75] For this reason, the central argument advanced by this book is that the discourse of development in Africa needs to be decolonized from its entrapment within the Euro-North American centric genealogy and must be epistemically reoriented within the Afrocentric paradigm to overthrow European hegemony.

Concluding Remarks

This book was guided by the paradigm of Afrocentricity as conceptualized by its leading theorist Molefi Kete Asante and the Temple University Circle of scholars. These scholars believe that the liberation of Africa and Africans in the continent and in the diaspora requires an unmasking of hegemonic cosmologies and their epistemic foundations as a way to end the domination of African people. They argue that unless Africans relocate epistemically to their own terms, grounded on their own understanding of historical and cultural experiences, and asserting their own agency, framed by cosmological, epistemological, axiological and aesthetic issues, they will remain the objects of Western development experimentation and subjugation. Thus, the proposition made by Afrocentricity is that Social Science Studies in general, and Development Studies in particular, must be re-examined from an African intellectual standpoint as a way to liberate Africans from colonial bondage. Asante suggests that 'African resurgence will never take place until Africans champion a renaissance grounded in a new paradigm of dramatic narratives of victory'.[76]

As a result of Eurocentric epistemic injustices, many analyses of development have been conceptually incapable of addressing the root causes of critical development problems in non-Western societies. Therefore, to escape from this impasse, African scholars must shift the geography of analysis to reflect on the historical journey that Africa has travelled. Therefore, understanding of Africa's development journey should not begin with the European invasion

75 Molefi Kete Asante, "African American Studies: The Future of the Discipline," *The Black Scholar* 22, no. 3 (1992): 23.

76 Asante, *African Pyramids of Knowledge*, 1.

of Africa, rather, it should go back to the entire history of Africa beginning with the Kemetic civilization along the Nile Valley. This would offer a more authentic assessment of the continent and its people. Africans must pursue in the most determined manner the practice of their renaissance, that is, a rebirth of the culture, philosophy, traditions and values of the continent, not in some antiquated form, but in the spirit of creative responses to contemporary times.[77] What African development discourses need is to foster a sensitivity to the African local context, which will assist in debunking the European hegemony. Development debates should not be formed via the direct transplantation of preconceived approaches; instead, they should be reconsidered in terms of African sociocultural, political, economic and environmental conditions.

We must caution against neoliberalism and its attempts to neutralize African demands for freedom. For too long, the West has sought to blame the African development impasse on African leaders themselves, accusing them of not implementing their prescriptions, as a way to exonerate themselves of the outcomes of their imperial global designs. The critical challenge facing African leaders and scholars is to deepen the revolution by demanding that Africa decolonize fully from the West – politically, economically, psychologically, spiritually and, most importantly, epistemically – and take its future into its own hands.

A Sesotho proverb proclaims: *Kopano ke Matla* (Unity is the Power).

77 Asante, *An Afrocentric Manifesto: Toward an African Renaissance*, 68.

BIBLIOGRAPHY

Adedeji, Adebayo. From the Lagos Plan of Action to the New Partnership for African Development and from the Final Act of Lagos to the Constitutive Act: Whither Africa? Keynote address at African Forum for Envisioning Africa, Nairobi, Kenya, 29 April 2002.

Adeleke, Tunda. "Africa and Afrocentric Historicism: A Critique." *Advances in Historical Studies* 4, no. 3 (2015): 200–15. https://doi.org/10.4236/ahs.2015.43016.

Adesina, Jimi O., Yao Graham, and Adebayo O. Olukoshi. *Africa and Development Challenges in the New Millennium: The NEPAD Debate*. London: Zed Books, 2006.

African Union. *Agenda 2063: The Africa We Want*. Addis Ababa: African Union Commission, 2015.

Alemazung, Joy Asongazoh. "Post-Colonial Colonialism: An Analysis of International Factors and Actors Marring African Socio-Economic and Political Development." *Journal of Pan African Studies* 3, no. 10 (2010): 62–84.

Alkebulan, Adisa A. "Defending the Paradigm." *Journal of Black Studies* 37, no. 3 (2007): 410–27.

Amin, Samir. *Eurocentricm*. New York, NY: Monthly Review Press, 1989.

Amin, Samir. *Maldevelopment: Anatomy of a Global Failure*. Tokyo and London: United Nations University Press and Zed Books, 1990.

Amin, Samir. *Eurocentrism: Modernity, Religion, and Democracy. A Critique of Eurocentrism and Culturalism*. New York, NY: Monthly Review Press, 2009.

Anderson, Tony. "Blowing Smoke: Exposing Empty Criticism of Afrocentricity." In *Molefi Kete Asante: In Praise and Criticism*, edited by Dhyana Ziegler, 115–24. Nashville, TN: Winston, 1995.

Ani, Marimba. *Yuguru: An Afrikan-centered Critique of European Cultural Thought and Behaviour*. Trenton, NJ: Africa World Press, 1994.

Araia, Ghelawdewos. *The Historical and Ideological Foundations of Pan-Africanism*. Institute of Development and Education for Africa. 2014. Accessed March 5, 2014, http://www.africanidea.org/pan-Africanism.html.

Arowolo, Dare. "The Effects of Western Civilization and Culture on Africa." *Afro-Asian Journal of Social Sciences* 1, no. 1 (Fourth Quarter, 2010): 1–14.

Asante, Molefi Kete. *Afrocentricity: The Theory of Social Change*. New York, NY: Amule, 1980.

Asante, Molefi Kete. *Afrocentricity*. Trenton, NJ: Africa World Press, 1988.

Asante, Molefi Kete. *Kemet, Afrocentricity, and Knowledge*. Trenton, NJ: Africa World Press, 1990.

Asante, Molefi Kete. "The Afrocentric Idea in Education." *Journal of Negro Education* 60 (1991): 170–9.

Asante, Molefi Kete. "African American Studies: The Future of the Discipline." *The Black Scholar* 22, no. 3 (1992): 20–29.

Asante, Molefi Kete. "The Principal Issues in Afrocentric Inquiry." In African Intellectual Heritage: A Book of Sources, edited by Molefi Kete Asante and Abu Shardow Abarry, 256–61. Philadelphia, PA: Temple University Press, 1996.

Asante, Molefi Kete. The Afrocentric Idea (revised and expanded edition). Philadelphia, PA: Temple University Press, 1998.

Asante, Molefi Kete. *The Painful Demise of Eurocentrism: An Afrocentric Response to Critics.* Trenton, NJ: Africa World Press, 1999.

Asante, Molefi Kete. "Afrocentricity and History: Mediating the Meaning of Culture in Western Society." *Souls: Critical Journal of Black Politics & Culture* 2, no. 3 (2000): 50–62.

Asante, Molefi Kete. *The Egyptian Philosophers: Ancient African Voices from Imhotep to Akhenaten.* Chicago, IL: African American Images, 2000.

Asante, Molefi Kete. "Locating the Eurocentric Assumptions about African History." In *Egypt vs. Greece and the American Academy: The Debate over the Birth of Civilization*, edited by Molefi Kete Asante, and Ama Mazama, 7–24. Chicago, IL: African American Images, 2002.

Asante, Molefi Kete. Afrocentricity: The Theory of Social Change (revised and expanded). Chicago, IL: African American Images, 2003.

Asante, Molefi Kete. *An Afrocentric Manifesto: Toward an African Renaissance.* Cambridge and Oxford: Polity Press, 2007.

Asante, Molefi Kete. Afrocentricity. 2009. http://www.asante.net/articles/1/afrocentricity.

Asante, Molefi Kete. *Facing South to Africa: Towards an Afrocentric Critical Orientation.* Lanham, MD: Lexington Books, 2014.

Asante, Molefi Kete. *African Pyramids of Knowledge: Kemet, Afrocentricity and Africology.* New York, NY: Universal Write Publications LLC, 2015.

Asante, Molefi Kete. "Afrocentricity and Knowledge: Adjusting the Narrative Lens." *The Thinker Magazine* 74 (2017): 24–6.

Asante, Molefi Kete. *Afrocentricity's Afrofuturism and the Countdown to the Future.* Conference paper delivered in Berlin, Germany, November 2–4, 2018.

Asante, Molefi Kete, and Abu Shardow Abarry. *African Intellectual Heritage: A Book of Sources.* Philadelphia, PA: Temple University Press, 1996.

Aziza, R. C. "The Relationship between Language Use and Survival of Culture: The Case of Umobo Youth." *Nigerian Language Studies* 4 (2001): 1–15.

Baah, Anthony. *History of African Development Initiatives.* Paper presented at the African Labour Research Network, Johannesburg, South Africa, 2003.

Baines, John. "Was Civilization Made in Africa?" *The New York Times Review of Books*, 1 (August 1, 1991): 12–13. https://www.nytimes.com/1991/08/11/books/was-civilization-made-in-africa.html.

Bakari, R. Sentwali. *Epistemology from an Afrocentric perspective: Enhancing Black Students' Consciousness through an Afrocentric Way of Knowing. Different Perspectives on Majority Rules*, 20. University of Nebraska-Lincoln, Lincoln, NB. 1997. https://digitalcommons.unl.edu/pocpwi2/20.

Baran, Paul A. *The Political Economy of Growth.* New York, NY: Monthly Review Press, 1957.

Bay, Mia. "The Historical Origins of Afrocentrism." *American Studies* 45, no. 4 (2000): 501–12.

Blaut, James Morris. *The Colonizer's Model of the World: Geographical Diffusion and Eurocentric History*. New York, NY: Guilford Press. 1993.

Breuilly, John. *Nationalism and the State*. Manchester: Manchester University Press, 1993.

Brohman, John. "Universalism, Eurocentrism, and Ideological Bias in Development Studies: From Modernisation to Neoliberalism." *Third World Quarterly* 16, no. 1 (1995): 121–40.

Bruton, Henry J. "The Search for a Development Economics." *World Development* 13, nos. 10–11 (1985): 1099–124.

Buch-Hansen, Mogens, and Laurids S. Lauridsen. "The Past, Present and Future of Develop-ment Studies." *Forum for Development Studies* 39, no. 3 (2012): 293–300. https://doi.org/10.1080/08039410.2012.709985.

Césaire, Aimé. *Discourse on Colonialism*. New York, NY: Monthly Review Press, 1955.

Chambers, Robert. *Rural Development: Putting the Last First*. Harlow: Prentice Hall, 1983.

Chatterjee, Partha. *Nationalist Thought and the Colonial World: A Derivative Discourse?* London: Zed Books, 1986.

Chawane, Midas. *The Development of Afrocentricity: A Historical Survey. Yesterday & Today*, 2016. http://www.sashtw.org.za/index2.htm.

Cheru, Fantu. "Development in Africa: The Imperial Project versus the National Project and the Need for Policy Space." *Review of African Political Economy* 120 (2009): 275–8.

Cherron, Inko-Tariah MBE. B: M2022. Dig Deep, Look Closer, Think Bigger: Black History Month Introductions. Downloaded from www.blackhistorymonth.org.uk on 25/10/2020.

Chivaura, Vimbai G., and Claude G. Mararike. *The Human Factor Approach to Development in Africa*. Harare: University of Zimbabwe Publications, 1998.

Chukwuokolo, J. Chodizie. "Afrocentrism or Eurocentrism: The Dilemma of African Development." *OGIRISI: New Journal of African Studies* 6, no. 1 (2009): 24–39.

Collins, Patricia Hill. *Black Feminist Thought*. New York, NY: Routledge, 1991.

Conrad, Joseph. *Heart of Darkness and Other Stories*. London: Wordsworth Editions, 1902.

Crouch, Stanley. "The Afrocentric Hustle." Journal of Blacks in Higher Education (Winter, 1995): 77–82.

Cullather, Nick. "Development Doctrine and Modernization Theory." In *Encyclopedia of American Foreign Policy*, New York, NY: Scribner, 2002.

Dabaghian, Jane. *Mirror of Man: Readings in Sociology and Literature*. Toronto: Little, Brown and Company, 1970.

Dastile, Nontyatyambo P. "Beyond Euro-Western Dominance: An African-Centred Decolonial Paradigm." *Africanus Journal of Development Studies* 43, no. 2 (2013): 93–104.

Davies, Carole Boyce. "Beyond Unicentricity: Transcultural Black Presences." *Research in African Literatures* 30, no. 2 (1999): 96–109.

Davis, Diane E. "Unlearning Languages of Development: From Rhetoric to Realism in Recent Studies of Latin America." *Latin American Research Review* 27 (1992): 151–68.

Diop, Cheikh Anta. *The African Origin of Civilization*. New York, NY: Lawrence Hill, 1974.

Diop, Cheikh Anta. *Civilization or Barbarism: An Authentic Anthropology*. New York, NY: Lawrence Hill, 1981.

Du Bois, W. E. B. (William Edward Burghardt). *The Souls of Black Folk: Essays and Sketches*. Chicago, IL: Lawrence Hill, 1903.

Early, Gerald, William.J. Moses, and Mary R. Lefkowitz. "Symposium: Historical Roots of Afrocentrism." *Academic Questions* 7, no. 2 (1994): 44–54.

Ekeh, Peter, *Colonialism and Social Structure: University of Ibadan Inaugural Lecture, 1980.* Ibadan: Ibadan University Press, 1983.

Ernest, John. Liberation Historiography: African American Writers and the Challenge of History, 1794–1861. Chapel Hill, NC: University of North Carolina Press, 2004.

Escobar, Arturo. *Encountering Development: The Making and Unmaking of the Third World* Princeton, NJ: Princeton University Press, 1995.

Esedebe, P. Olisanwuche. *Pan-Africanism: The Idea and the Movement, 1776–1963.* Washington, DC: Howard University Press, 1970.

Estera, G. 1996 "Development." In The Development Dictionary: A Guide to Knowledge as Power, edited by Wolfgang E. Sachs, 7. London: Zed Books, 1996, 1–306.

Esteva, Gustavo, and Madhu Suri Prakash. "Beyond Development, What?" *Development in Practice* 8, no. 3 (1998), 280–96.

Edward, Ezedike. *African Culture and the African Personality. From Footmarks to Landmarks on African Philosophy.* Somolu: Obaroh and Ogbinaka Publishers, 2009.

Fage, John D. *A History of West Africa: An Introductory Survey.* London: Oxford University Press, 1969.

Fanon, Frantz. *The Wretched of the Earth.* New York, NY: Grove Press, 1968.

Ferguson, James. *The Anti-Politics Machine:* "Development", *Depoliticization, and Bureaucratic Power in Lesotho.* Cambridge: Cambridge University Press, 1990.

Finch, Charles, III. "Critiquing the Critics: Advancing the Paradigm." In *Egypt vs. Greece and the American Academy: The Debate over the Birth of Civilization*, edited by Molefi Kete Asante, and Ama Mazama, 37–50. Chicago, IL: African American Images, 2002.

Gbotokuma, Zeke. "Cultural Identity and Underdevelopment in sub-Saharan Africa." *Voices from Africa*, 4 (1996): 17–29.

Gordon, Jacob. "Towards an African Historiography." In *Egypt vs. Greece and the American Academy: The Debate over the Birth of Civilization*, edited by Molefi Kete Asante, and Ama Mazama, 25–36. Chicago, IL: African American Images, 2002.

Gordon, Lewis R. *An Introduction to Africana Philosophy.* New York, NY: Cambridge University Press, 2008.

Grosfoguel, Ramón. "The Epistemic Decolonial Turn: Beyond Political-Economy Paradigms." *Cultural Studies* 21, nos. 2–3 (2007): 211–23.

Grosfoguel, Ramón. "Decolonizing Post-Colonial Studies and Paradigms of Political Economy: Transmodernity, Decolonial Thinking, and Global Coloniality." Transmodernity*: Journal of Peripheral Cultural Production of the Luso-Hispanic World* 1, no. 1 (2011): 1–34.

Gunn, Jean Philippe. "African Nationalism from the Colonial Period to the Post-Colonial Period." *Social Sciences Studies Journal* 4, no. 20 (2018): 2988–95.

Gwekwerere, Tavengwa. "From Nat Turner to Molefi Asante: Reading the European Intellectual Indictment of the Afrocentric Conception of Reality." *Journal of Black Studies* 41, no. 1 (2010): 108–26. https://doi.org/10.1177/0021934708328249.

Hall, Stephen G. A Faithful Account of the Race: African American Historical Writing in 19th *Century America.* Chapel Hill, NC: University of North Carolina Press, 2009.

Hardt, Michael, and Antonio Negri. *Empire.* Cambridge, MA: Harvard University Press, 2000.

Hegel, Georg Wilhelm Friedrich. The Philosophy of History, translated by J. Sibree. New York: Dover, 1956.

Hettne, Bjorn. "The Development of Development Theory." Acta Sociologica 26, nos. 3/4 (1983): 247–66.

Hettne, Bjorn. *Development Theory and the Three Worlds: Towards an International Political Economy of Development* (2nd ed.). Harlow and New York, NY: Longman, 1995.

Hilliard, Asa G., III. "Bridging Maat, Destroying Isfet: The African and African Diasporian Presence in the Study of Ancient Kmt." In Egypt: Child of Africa, edited by Ivan van Sertima, 127–48. New Brunswick, NJ: Transaction Publishers, 1995.

Hilliard, Asa G., III. "The Myth of the Immaculate Conception of Western Civilization." In Egypt vs. Greece and the American Academy: The Debate over the Birth of Civilization, edited by Molefi Kete Asante, and Ama Mazama, 51–66. Chicago, IL: African American Images, 2002.

Hume, David. "Of National Characters." In *Essays, Moral, Political and Literary.* Harmondsworth: Penguin, [1748] 1969.

Ibhawoh, Bonny and Jeremiah Dibua. "Deconstructing *Ujamaa*: The Legacy of Julius Nyerere in the Quest for Social and Economic Development in Africa." *African Journal of Political Science* 8 (2003): 59–82.

Ikome, Francis Nguendi. *From LPA to NEPAD: The Political Economy of African Regional Initiatives.* Midrand: Institute for Global Dialogue, 2007.

Jackson, Ronald L. and Michael A. Hogg (eds.). *Encyclopaedia of Identity: Afrocentricity.* Thousand Oaks, CA: Sage, 2010.

James, George G. M. Stolen Legacy. New York, NY: Classic House Books, [1954] 2009.

Karenga, Maulana. *Introduction to Black Studies* (3rd ed). Los Angeles, CA: University of Sankore Press, 2002.

Karenga, Maulana. *Maat: The Moral Ideal in Ancient Egypt.* Los Angeles, CA: University of Sankore Press, 2006.

Kaunda, Kenneth D., and Colin M. Morris. *A Humanist in Africa: Letters to Colin M. Morris from Kenneth D. Kaunda, President of Zambia.* Nashville, TN and New York, NY: Abingdon Press, 1966.

Keita, Maghan. *Race and the Writing of History: Riddling the Sphinx.* New York, NY: Oxford University Press, 2000.

Keto, C. Tsehloane. *The African Centered Perspective of History.* Blackwood, NJ: K. A. Publications, 1989.

Khokholkova, Nadezdha. "Afrocentricity: The Evolution of the Theory in the Context of American History." *Social Evolution and History* 15, no. 1 (2016): 111–25.

Langdon, Jonathan. "Decolonizing Development Studies: Reflections on Critical Pedagogies in Action." *Canadian Journal of Development Studies* 34, no. 3 (2013): 384–99. https://doi.org/10.1080/02255189.2013.825205.

Lefkowitz, Mary. *Not Out of Africa: How Afrocentrism Became an Excuse to Teach Myth as History.* New York, NY: Basic Books, 1996.

Legum, Colin. *Pan-Africanism: A Short Political Guide.* New York, NY: Frederick A. Praeger, 1965.

Lerner, Daniel. *The Passing of Traditional Society: Modernizing the Middle East.* Glencoe, IL: Free Press, 1958.

Lubieniecka, Ewelina Róża. *Does Post-Development Theory Find Alternatives to Westernization of International Relations? African Perspective.* The 8th Pan-European Conference on International Relations. Poland: University of Warsaw, 2013.

Luke, Don E. "Preserving the Euro-supremacist Myth." In Egypt vs. Greece and the American Academy: The Debate over the Birth of Civilization, edited by Molefi Kete Asante, and Ama Mazama, 91–120. Chicago, IL: African American Images, 2002.

Lushaba, Lwazi Siyabonga. *Development as Modernity, Modernity as Development.* Dakar: CODESRIA, 2009.

Mafeje, Archibald. "Africanity: A Combative Ontology." CODESRIA Bulletin 1 & 4 (2000): 66–71.

Maldonado-Torres, Nelson. "On the Coloniality of Being." *Cultural Studies,* 21, nos. 2–3 (2007): 240–70.

Matunhu, Jephias. "A Critique of Modernization and Dependency Theories in Africa: Critical Assessment." *African Journal of History and Culture* 3, no. 5 (2011): 65–67.

Mazama, Ama. "The Afrocentric Paradigm: Contours and Definitions." *Journal of Black Studies* 31, no. 4 (2001): 387–405.

Mazama, Ama. *The Afrocentric Paradigm.* Trenton, NJ: Africa World Press, 2003.

Mazama, Ama. *Afrocentricity and the Critical Question of African Agency,* 2014, https://www.dyabukam.com/index.php/en/knowledge/philosophy/item/136-afrocentricity.

Mazrui, Ali A. *The Africans: A Triple Heritage.* London: BBC Publication, 1986.

Mazrui, Ali A. "The Re-invention of Africa: Edward Said, V. Y. Mudimbe, and Beyond." *Research in African Literatures* 3, no. 36 (2005): 68–82.

Mbakogu, Ifeyinwa Annastasia. "Is There Really a Relationship Between Culture and Development?" *Anthropology* 6, no. 1 (2004): 37–43. https://doi.org/10.1080/09720073.2004.11890827.

Mbeki, Thabo. Address by Executive Deputy President Thabo Mbeki, to Corporate Council on Africa's "Attracting Capital" Summit, Chantilly VA, 19–22 April 1997. South African History Online. Accessed February 2, 2020, http://www.dirco.gov.za (accessed 2 February 2020).

Mehmet, Ozay. *Westernizing the Third World: The Eurocentricity of Economic Development Theories.* London and New York, NY: Routledge, 1995.

Mignolo, Walter D. *The Idea of Latin America.* Malden, MA: Blackwell, 2005.

Mignolo, Walter D. "Introduction: Coloniality of Power and Decolonial Thinking." *Cultural Studies* 21, nos. 2–3 (2007): 155–67.

Mkandawire, Thandika. "Running While Others Walk: Knowledge and the Challenge of Africa's Development." *Africa Development* 26, no. 2 (2011): 1–36.

Moloi, Lehasa R. "An Afrocentric Development Paradigm: A Model that Matters for Africa." In Reinventions and Contestations of Thought-power: Emerging Perspectives on Pan-Africanism, edited by Percy-Sledge Chigora, Richard R. Mahomva, and Majahana Lunga, 120–35. Harare: LAN Readers, 2018.

Monteiro-Ferreira, Ana. "Afrocentricity and the Western Paradigm." *Journal of Black Studies,* 40, no. 2 (2014): 327–36.

Monteiro-Ferreira, Ana. *The Demise of the Inhumane: Afrocentricity, Modernism, and Postmodernism.* Albany, NY: Sunny Press, 2014.

Mudimbe, Valentin Y. *The Invention of Africa: Gnosis, Philosophy and the Order of Knowledge.* Indianapolis, IN: Indiana University Press, 1988.

Namkoong, Young. "Dependency Theory: Concepts, Classification, and Criticism." *International Study Review* 2, no. 1 (1999):121–50. https://doi.org/10.1177/223386599900200106.

Ndlovu-Gatsheni, Sabelo J. Coloniality of Power in Development Studies and the Impact of Global Imperial Designs. Inaugural lecture, Pretoria: UNISA, AMRI, 2012.

Ndlovu-Gatsheni, Sabelo J. "The Entrapment of Africa within the Global Colonial Matrices of Power: Eurocentrism, Coloniality, and Deimperialization in the Twenty-First Century." *Journal of Developing Societies* 29, no. 4 (2013): 331–53.

Ndlovu-Gatsheni, Sabelo J. "Decoloniality as the Future of Africa." *History Compass* 13, no. 10 (2015): 485–96.

Ndlovu-Gatsheni, Sabelo J. "The African Idea of Development." In *Routledge Handbook of African Development*, edited by Tony Binns, Kenneth Lynch, and Etienne Nel, 1–16. London: Routledge, 2017.

Ndlovu-Gatsheni, Sabelo J. *Epistemic Freedom in Africa: Deprovincialization and Decolonization*. London: Routledge, 2018.

Ndlovu-Gatsheni, Sabelo J. "Revisiting the African Renaissance." In *Oxford Research Encyclopedia*. Oxford: Oxford University Press, 2019.

Ngugi wa Thiong'o. *Moving the Centre: The Struggle for Cultural Freedoms*. London: James Currey, 1993.

Ngugi wa Thiong'o. *Something Torn and New: An African Renaissance*. New York, NY: Basic Civitas Books, 2009.

Ngugi wa Thiong'o. *Re-membering Africa*. Nairobi: East African Publishers, 2009.

Ngugi wa Thiong'o. *Globaletics: Theory and the Politics of Knowing*. New York, NY: Columbia University Press, 2012.

Nkrumah, Kwame. *Africa Must Unite*. London: PANAF, 1963.

Nkrumah, Kwame. *Neo-Colonialism: The Last Stage of Imperialism*. London: PANAF, 1965.

Nwala, T. Uzodinma. Critical Review of the Great Debate on African Philosophy (1970–1990). Ntsukka: William Amo Centre for African Philosophy UNN, 1992.

Obenga, Theophile. "Thales of Miletus and Egypt." In Egypt vs. Greece *and the American Academy: The Debate over the Birth of Civilization*, edited by Molefi Kete Asante, and Ama Mazama, 165–84. Chicago, IL: African American Images, 2002.

Olusoga, David. "The Roots of European Racism Lie in the Slave Trade, Colonialism – and Edward Long." *The Guardian*, September 8, 2015, https://www.theguardian.com/commentisfree/2015/sep/08/european-racism-africa-slavery.

Olutayo, Akinpelu Olanrewaju. "Gender, Society and Development." In *Nigerian Life and Culture: A Book of Readings*, edited by Olatunji Y. Oyeneye and Moses O. Shoremi, 190–208. Ago-Iwoyi: Ogun State University, 1985.

Omari, T. Peter. *Kwame Nkrumah: The Anatomy of an African Dictatorship*. New York, NY: Africana Publishing Corporation, 1970.

Onyenuru, Okechukwu P. *Mudimbe on European Account of the African* (pp. 1–13). Ibadan: Dominican Institute, Samanda, Nigeria, 2014.

Owens, Michael Eric. *Yes, I Am Who I Am: A New Philosophy of Black Identity*. Tulsa, OK: Yorkshire Publishing, 2009.

Padmore, George. *Pan-Africanism or Communism*. New York, NY: Double-Day Anchor, 1972.

Perron, Pierre. "The Great Crash, the Oil Price Shock, and the Unit Root Hypothesis." *Econometrica* 57, no. 6 (1989): 1361–401.

Pieterse, Jan Nederveen. "Dilemmas of Development Discourse: The Crisis of Developmentalism and the Comparative Method." *Development and Change* 22 (1991): 1–17.

Pieterse, Jan Nederveen. *My Paradigm or Yours? Alternative Development, Post-Development, Reflexive Development*. Institute of Social Studies: Working Paper Series No. 229, 1996.

Plaatjie, Sebeka Richard. "Beyond Western-centric and Eurocentric Development: A Case for Decolonizing Development." *Africanus Journal of Development Studies* 43, no. 2 (2013): 118–30. https://doi.org/10.25159/0304-615X/2306.

Plato. *The Republic*, X, 600A [ca 375 BCE].

Prah, Kwesi Kwaa. *The Afrocentric Nation: The State of the Nation.* Cape Town: Centre for Advanced Studies of African Society, 2006.

Quijano, Anibal. "The Coloniality of Power and Social Classification." *Journal of World Systems* 6, no. 2 (2000): 342–86.

Regan, Clara, Bertrand Borg, and Tony Meade (eds.). *80:20 Development in an Unequal World.* Bray: 80:20 Educating and Acting for a Better World Publishing, 2006.

Richburg, Keith B. *Out of America: A Black Man Confronts Africa.* New York, NY: Basic Books, 1996.

Rist, Gilbert. *The History of Development: From Western Origin to Global Faith.* London: Zed Books, 2002.

Rodney, Walter. *How Europe Underdeveloped Africa.* London: Bogle-L'Ouverture, 1972.

Rostow, Walt W. *The Stages of Economic Growth.* Cambridge: Cambridge University Press, 1960.

Sachs, Wolfgang E. *The Development Dictionary: A Guide to Knowledge as Power.* Johannesburg: Witwatersrand University Press, 1992.

Senghor, Leopold S. *On African Socialism.* Translated with an introduction by Mercer Cook. London: Pall Mall Press, [1959] 1964.

Shavit, Yaacov. *History in Black: African-Americans in Search of an Ancient Past.* London: Frank Cass, 2001.

Smedley, Audrey. *Race in North America: The Origins and Evolution of a Worldview.* Boulder, CO: Westview, 1993.

Smith, Anthony Douglas. *Theories of Nationalism.* London: Gerald Duckworth, 1971.

Stewart, Peter, and Moipane Rakologane. *Development Theories: Only Study Guide for DVA3701.* Pretoria: UNISA, 2016.

Stiglitz, Joseph E. *Globalization and Its Discontents.* New York, NY: Norton, 2002.

Sumner, Andrew. "What Is Development Studies?" *Development in Practice* 16, no. 6 (2006): 644–50. https://doi.org/10.1080/09614520600958363.

Sylvester, Christine. "Development Studies and Postcolonial Studies: Disparate Tales of the 'Third World'." *Third World Quarterly* 20, no. 4 (1999): 703–21. https://doi.org/10.1080/01436599913514.

Talton, Benjamin. *The Challenge of Decolonization in Africa,* 2017, accessed February 9, 2018, http://onlinetuit.blogspot.co.za/2017/02/the-challenge-of-decolonization-in.html.

Taylor, Lance. "Editorial: The Revival of the Liberal Creed – the IMF and the World Bank in a Globalized Economy." *World Development* 25, no. 2 (1997): 145–52.

Therien, Jean-Philippe. "Beyond the North-South Divide: The Two Tales of World Poverty." *Third World Quarterly* 20, no. 4 (1999): 723–42.

Trevor-Roper, Hugh. *The Rise of Christian Europe.* London: Jarrold and Sons, 1967.

Truman, Harry S. *Point Four.* Inaugural Address, 1949, http://www.bartleby.com/124/pres53.html.

Verharen, Charles C. "Molefi Asante and an Afrocentric Curriculum," *Western Journal of Black Studies* 24, no. 4 (2000): 223–38.

Verharen, Charles C. "In and Out of Africa: Misreading Afrocentricity." In *Egypt vs. Greece and the American Academy: The Debate over the Birth of Civilization,* edited by Molefi Kete Asante, and Ama Mazama, 67–90. Chicago, IL: African American Images, 2002.

Villa-Vicencio, Charles, Eric Doxtader, and Ebrahim Moosa. *The African Renaissance and the Afro-Arab Spring: A Season of Rebirth?* Cape Town: University of Cape Town Press, 2015.

Viriri, Advice, and Pascah Mungwini. "African Cosmology and the Duality of Western Hegemony: The Search for African Identity," *Journal of Pan African Studies* 3, no. 6 (March 2010): 27–42.

Wagner, Roy. *The Invention of Culture.* Chicago, IL and London: University of Chicago Press, 1981.

Walker, Clarence E. *Why We Can't Go Home Again: An Argument about Afrocentrism.* New York, NY: Oxford University Press, 2001.

Wallerstein, Immanuel. *The Modern World System: Capitalist Agriculture and the Origin of the European World-Economy in the Sixteenth Century.* New York, NY: Academic Press, 1974.

Weber, Max. *The Protestant Ethic and the Spirit of Capitalism.* New York, NY: Charles Scribner and Sons, 1958.

Welsh-Asante, Kariamu. *The African Aesthetic: Keeper of the Traditions.* Westport, CT: Praeger, 1994.

Winters, Clyde A. "Ancient Afrocentric History and the Genetic Model." In *Egypt vs. Greece and the American Academy: The Debate over the Birth of Civilization*, edited by Molefi Kete Asante, and Ama Mazama, 121–64. Chicago, IL: African American Images, 2002.

Woodson, Carter G. *The Miseducation of the Negro.* Washington, DC: Associated Press, 1933.

INDEX

Abarry 101
acculturation 37, 96
Adedeji, Adebayo 57, 111
Adeleke 37, 38
aesthetics 22, 23, 104, 107, 109
Africa-centredness 61
African agency 43, 107, 108, 110, 115, 117, 120
  concept of 107
  denial of 106, 114
  political strategy to deny 41
  re-assertion of 72
  role of 105
  significance of 40
African Americans 28, 38, 115
African context 1, 7, 13, 23, 46
African culture 19, 21, 22, 29, 88, 90, 92, 93, 98, 104
African decolonization 16, 85, 120
African development 5, 7, 9, 59, 110, 111, 112
  agenda 62
  contribution to 65
  debates 98
  initiatives 1
  paradigm 87
  perspective 94
  search for 80
African development challenge 81, 84
African development discourse 43, 88, 107, 122
African development impasse 111, 122
African development trajectory 59, 98, 111
African history 41, 68, 79, 80, 82, 97
  classical 75
  context of 98, 113, 115
  distortion 93
  Eurocentric narratives about 73
  falsify 74
  narration of 31, 32
  perspective on 29
  retelling of 71
  rewriting of 30, 65
  role of 66
  study of 72
  understanding of 75
African history and culture 1, 15, 71, 80, 81, 93
  European account of 93
  misrepresention 94
  reclaiming 92
African Intellectual Heritage: A Book of Sources 67, 101
African nationalism 34, 105, 109, 115, 117–21
African ontological density 16, 100, 108
African people 9, 24, 73, 112, 113, 117–19
  aesthetics of 22, 110
  best interest of 23
  collective story of 22
  cultural narratives of 59
  cultural unity of the 75
  dehumanization of 58
  dislocation of 2, 87
  domination of 121
  history and culture of 13
  humanity of 69, 109
  invalidate 31
  lived experiences of 15, 17, 97
  quality of life 16
  re-ground 7, 19
  restoration of 18, 108
  subjugation of 40, 83
  values of 69, 91

African perspective 16
African phenomena 15, 17, 21, 73, 81
African reclamation 92
African renaissance 74, 81, 82, 84, 109
 concept of 81
 crystallization of the 85
 future of the 83
 paradigm of 66, 108
 pursuit of an 72, 80
 resource for an 118
 search for an 73, 85
 source for an 75
 struggle for 84
African Renaissance 81, 83
African resurgence 59, 107, 121
African revitalization 84
African socialism 55
African-based
 development initiatives 6
 knowledge system 15
African-centred worldview 24
Africology 8, 15, 25, 73
Afro-Arab Spring 86
Afro-Asiatic solidarity 57
Afrocentric
 approach 18
 awakening 14
 development paradigm 62, 64, 105
 historicism 29, 37, 39, 65, 72
 historiography 66, 71–73
 history 29
 movement 35
 perspective 3, 6, 19, 64
 research 22, 24
 theory 27, 28
Afrocentric Greek dependency theory 37
The Afrocentric Paradigm 99
Afrocentricity 7, 22, 39, 40, 121
 concept of 17
 consciousness as a 98
 critics of 37, 39, 41
 cultural criticism 9
 definition 17, 115
 deployment of 2
 development of 26, 73
 emergence of 18, 26
 essence of 22
 ethical intellectual standpoint 59
 focal point 23
 goal of 24, 32
 historical claims of 36
 historical roots of 24
 leitmotifs of 29
 moral aesthetics of 82
 paradigm as a 1, 16, 17, 25, 81, 109, 121
 primary objective of 15, 20
 proponents of 41
 qualitative nature of 9
 revolutionary paradigm 7, 97
 theory of 3, 5, 7, 29, 66, 113
Afrocentricity: The Theory of Social Change 17, 25, 120
Afrocentrism 35, 36, 39, 40
 criticism of 40
Afrocentrist 6, 9, 21–24, 26, 32, 36, 73, 74
 objective of 32
Alemazung 54, 56
alternative humanist development strategies 57
Amin, Samir 3, 46, 92
Anaximander 78
Anaximenes of Miletus 78
ancient Egyptians 60, 69, 73, 75, 77, 80
Ani, Marimba 87
anti-politics machine 46
apartheid 44, 55, 80, 109
Arusha Declaration (Tanzania) 56
Asante, Molefi Kete 1, 6, 9, 15–16, 23, 24, 73, 88–94, 96, 98–100, 107–8, 115, 118–21
axiology 23

Baah, Anthony 13, 53, 57
Baines, John 77
Balkanization 118
Bandung Conference 57, 59, 62, 109
barbarism 31, 33, 51, 69
Berlin Conference 5, 34, 54, 63, 80, 82, 91, 106, 112
Berlin Scramble 54, 60, 112
Black Consciousness Movement 7
black racist historiography 37
Boukman, Dutty 116
Bretton Woods Institutions 57, 59, 111

Bretton Woods paradigm of development 58, 111
Brohman, John 12, 44, 95, 96, 103
Bruton, Henry J 88
Burton, Richard 68

capitulationists 41
Césaire, Aimé 26, 52
Chambers, Robert 9, 64
Chawane, Midas 27, 29, 33, 34, 41
Cheru, Fantu 7, 48, 84
Christianity 48, 67, 69
Chukwuokolo, J. Chodizie 13, 24, 32, 62, 69
Civil Rights Movement 7
Civilization or Barbarism: An Authentic Anthropology 75
Cold War 57
Collins, Patricia Hill 27
colonial
  culture 26, 92, 108
  dismemberment 14
  domination 73, 104, 108, 109, 115
  education 100, 106
  enterprise 34, 91, 92
  epistemicides 86
  framework 45
  knowledge system 16
  legacy 53
  matrices of power 4, 46
  oppression 6, 33, 117
  perspective 48, 67
colonialism 44, 82, 83, 92, 101, 119, 120
  domination 62
  effects of 61
  legacy 80
  long-term effects of 63
  process 33
coloniality 3–5, 12, 46, 48, 57, 62, 66, 118
  logic of 71, 102, 111
coloniality-anchored perspectives 51
colonization of Africa 15, 43, 70, 89
colonization of knowledge 5
Common Man's Charter (Uganda) 56
Conrad, Joseph 49
control mechanisms
  African economy 5
  control of authority 5
  control of gender and sexuality 5
  control of subjectivities and knowledge 5
cultural bias 52, 95
cultural ethnocentrism 93
cultural imperialism 87–89
culture
  concept of 89, 90
  material aspects of 90

Dakar meeting 81
Damas, Leon 26
Davis, Diane E., 12
debt dependency 85
declarations 56, 84
decolonization 2, 4, 6, 13, 44, 53, 54, 57, 66, 82, 92, 98, 109, 118
  of Development Studies 2
decolonization project 4
dehumanization 34, 55
democratization 58, 86
dependency theorists 11, 50
developmentalism 48, 49, 53, 102, 111
dictatorial regimes 86
Diop, Cheikh Anta 26, 27, 66, 73, 76, 81
Diopian historiography 26, 75
Diopian view 75
Discourse on Colonialism 52
dismemberment 60, 80, 84, 105
  African 46, 82
djed 72, 83, 92, 115
Du Bois, W.E.B., 27, 28, 37, 72, 75, 85, 96, 116, 117

East African Community (EAC) 57
Economic Community of West African States (ECOWAS) 57
economic decolonization 85, 118
economic structural adjustment policies (ESAPs) 12
Egypt 30, 75, 78, 79, 86
Egyptian
  civilization 35, 77
  influence 80
  priests 78
Egyptians 31, 32, 36, 75, 76, 79
Ekeh, Peter 33, 44
Encountering Development The Making and Unmaking of the Third World 102
enlightenment 30, 46, 47, 70, 84, 102
enlightenment movement 106

enslavement 16, 28, 44, 55, 58, 80, 109
epistemic justice 6, 7
epistemic racism 2, 7, 13, 24, 29, 44, 99
epistemological decolonization 86
epistemological ethnocentrism 93
epistemology
  African 22, 115
  African-centred 1
  alterity 13, 64
  decolonization of 3
  Eurocentric 1, 96, 98
  European colonial 6
  geography of 3
  historical 26
  liberation of 16
  Western 12, 43
Escobar, Arturo 13, 45, 52, 95, 102, 103
Esteva, Gustavo 45, 52
ethnocentric view 62, 99
ethnocentrism 93
Euro-American racism 117
Euro-centredness 61, 64
Eurocentric
  bias 12, 13, 30, 97
  dominance 19, 21
  hegemony 17, 22–24
  historiography 16, 66
  narrative 3, 47, 48
  paradigm 15, 75
  perspective 20, 46
  racism 31
  scholar 21, 28, 35, 36, 39, 75, 76, 79, 100
  standards 49, 59, 62
  standards of modernity 59
  supremacist 19
  worldview 21
Eurocentric ideological framework 1, 106
Eurocentric models
  parochial 1
Eurocentric modernist paradigm 10
Eurocentric view 59, 62, 94, 99
Eurocentrism 3, 6, 8, 14, 18, 59, 62, 80, 88, 92
  criticism 19
  in Development Studies 43
  domination 25
  epistemic implications of 46
  ethnocentric 113
  negative impact of 5
Euro-modernity ix, 92
Euro-North American agenda 9
Euro-North American-centric agenda 6
European colonization 5, 33, 50, 64, 67, 89, 106
European cultural imperialism 88
European dominance 21, 94
  legacy of 54
European domination 11, 19, 34, 97, 105, 107, 114, 115, 117, 120
European Enlightenment project 1
European hegemonic standards 51
European historiography 28
European modernity 55, 73
European modernization 83, 89
European political hegemony 16
European racial superiority 31
European scholarship 22, 30, 71
European slave trade 72
European-designed development experiments 88
Europeanised Loyalists 41
Euro-supremacy mythology 70, 71
exogenous process 10
Ezedike, E. O., 90

Fage, John D., 68
failure to develop 58
Fanon, Frantz 54
Ferguson, James 45
financial rescue packages 56
Finch III, Charles 78
fiscal austerity 58
free market ideology 57
Freedom Charter (South Africa) 56

Garvey, Marcus 65, 85, 110, 117
geometry of Pythagoras 79
Global North 4, 5, 18, 19, 48, 50
  domination agenda 1
Global South 3, 4, 7, 10, 11, 44, 46–50, 53, 97, 110, 111
Gordon, Lewis R., 39
Greece 31, 32, 35, 37, 41, 68, 72, 74–76, 78
Greek civilization 36, 77, 78, 80
Greek mathematics 79

Greek philosophy 36, 78
Greeks 32, 36, 77, 80
Gwekwerere, Tavengwa 40

Haitian Revolution 84, 116
heart of darkness 49, 67
Hegel, Georg Wilhelm Friedrich 31, 69, 90
Heraclitus of Ephesus 78
Hettne, Bjorn 11
Hilliard, Asa G., 40
History in Black African Americans in Search of Their Past 35
holism 22
How Europe Underdeveloped Africa 51
Human Development Index (HDI) 61
human factor approach 61
human-centred approach to development 56
human-centred development 55
humanism 55
  African 55
Hume, David 33

Ikome, Francis Nguendi 58
imperialism 34, 44, 48, 52, 55, 58, 67, 80
inferiority complex 5
International Monetary Fund (IMF) 57, 85, 111
Isocrates the Ionian 78

James, George G.M., 36, 75, 77
just distribution of wealth 58

Karenga, Maulana 26, 27, 78
Kaunda, Kenneth 55, 56
Kawaida 26, 27
Kawaida communitarian philosophy 26
Kawaidan philosophy 27
Keita, Maghan 38
Kemet 18, 24, 74, 76, 79, 80
Kemet (Egypt) 16, 59, 75
Kemetic civilization 122
Kemites 60
Keto, C. Tsehloane 72
Khokholkova, Nadezdha 27

Lagos Plan of Action (LPA) 58
Langdon, Jonathan 2, 11
Lefkowitz, Mary R., 36, 41, 77
legitimization of violence 5
Legum, Colin 116, 117
Lerner, Daniel 10, 48
liberalization 58
life expectancy 61
Litwack, Leon 71
location of phenomena 9
Louverture,Toussaint 116
Lushaba, Lwazi Siyabonga 12, 49, 60, 102

Maat 78
Mafeje, Archibald 13, 28, 64
marginalization 21, 53, 55, 108
  African 56
Marxists 41
Maskers 41
Mazama, Ama 8, 19, 20, 22–25, 73, 106, 113, 118
Mazrui, Ali A 63, 106
Mbakogu, Ifeyinwa Annastasia 89, 91, 103
Mbeki, Thabo 83
Mehmet, Ozay 53
Middle Passage 29
Mkandawire, Thandika 49, 88
modernist-elitist models 53
modernity 3, 12, 46
modernization 13, 43, 49, 61, 67, 95, 97, 103, 120
modernization approach 97
modernization model 61
modernization paradigm 1, 10, 55
modernization project 11, 46
modernization theory 11, 49–51, 61, 62, 87, 95, 105, 106
Monteiro-Ferreira, Ana 17, 73, 99, 100, 114
Moving the Centre The Struggle for Cultural Freedoms 64
Mudimbe, Valentin Y., 93, 95
Mulugushi Declaration (Zambia) 56

Namkoong, Young 11
Ndlovu-Gatsheni, Sabelo J., 3, 4, 12, 16, 44, 46, 53, 55, 63, 80, 85, 95, 102
négritude 26
neo-colonial oppression 103
neo-colonialism 4, 44, 54, 55, 80, 83–85, 102, 109, 118

Neo-colonialism The Last Stage of Imperialism 54
neoliberal development thinking 97
neo-liberalism 43, 44, 80
New International Economic Order (NIEO) 109
Ngugi wa Thiong'o 55, 60, 64, 82, 84
Nile Valley 16, 68, 73, 75, 76, 78, 79, 82, 118, 122
Nkrumah, Kwame 4, 54, 56, 66, 71, 82, 84, 85, 102, 117
non-Western societies 13, 44, 96, 97, 101, 106, 121
Not Out of Africa 77
Nubian 22
Nyerere, Julius 56, 71, 103, 110

One-Centeredness 47
Organization of African Unity (OAU) 53, 117

The Painful Demise of Eurocentrism An Afrocentric Response to Critics 41
Pan-African congress 116, 117
Pan-Africanism 34, 37, 70, 85, 105, 106, 108, 109, 115–18, 120, 121
Pan-Africanism and identity paradigm 37
pan-Negro movement 116
parochial European perspective 106
parochialism 18
Philosophy of History 31
Pieterse, Jan Nederveen 50
Plaatjie, Sebeka Richard 51
Plato 78, 79
Point Four programme 60, 111
political decolonization 84, 85, 118
political kingdom 84, 118
postcolonial administration 53
postcolonial era 53, 63
post-colonial political order 4
post-enlightenment 48
post-independence era 14, 16, 45, 53, 54, 82, 112, 113, 119, 120
post-World War II 48, 52, 57, 83
post-World War II development vision 111
Prakash, Madhu Suri 45, 52
pre-colonial era 62
Preston, P. W., 112
primitivism 47, 52
privatization 11, 58
pseudohistory 35

Quijano, Anibal 3, 4

racism 25, 28, 29, 32, 51, 56, 71, 105, 114
racist Eurocentric scholarship 29, 31
re-membering 55, 60, 64, 84
resurgence of Africa 80, 82
Revised framework for principles of the new international order in Africa 58
Rhind mathematical papyrus 80
Rhodes Must Fall 86
Rist, Gilbert 12
Rodney, Walter 51

Sachs, Wolfgang E., 13
Scramble for Africa 5, 34, 54, 63, 80
Senghor, Léopold S., 23, 26
Shavit, Yaacov 35, 37, 41
slave trade 34, 48, 63, 67
social revolution 56
Stolen Legacy 36
stolen legacy theory 37
Structural Adjustment Programmes 85
Sumner, Andrew 3

Temple Circle of Afrocentric scholarship 90
Temple University Circle of scholars 8, 92, 121
Thales 78
theory of value (*see* axiology)
Therien, Jean-Philippe 58
Third World 3, 10, 12, 44, 52, 53, 58, 103
traditionalism 52
Transatlantic slave trade 28, 29, 33
Travels in Arabia and Africa (1866) 68
Trevor-Roper, Hugh 69
Truman, Harry S., 48, 60, 84, 94, 102, 111

Ujamaa 55, 56
unicentricity 47
United Nations Development Programme 61
United Nations Educational, Scientific, and Cultural Organization (UNESCO) 103
universalism 41, 44, 99, 109

Von Humboldt,Wilhelm and
Alexander 33
voyages of discovery 1, 48, 67

Wagner, Roy 94
Washington Consensus 44, 55, 58, 80, 112
Weber, Max 69
Western agenda 44
Western centrism 8
Western dominance 12
Western epistemological hegemony 2
Western modernity 50
Westphalian Peace Treaty 112
white gaze 3, 7
white racial domination 24, 108, 114
white racial dominion 18
white supremacist 6, 41, 88
white supremacy 25, 100
Winters, Clyde A., 75–77
Woodson, Carter G., 72, 100
World Bank 57, 85, 111
World Trade Organization 111
World War II 1, 10, 11, 43, 60, 67, 87, 94,
101, 105, 109
Wright, W.D., 37

Yoruba 22
Yuguru: An Afrikan-Centered Critique of European Cultural Thought and Behaviour 88

Zulu 22

www.ingramcontent.com/pod-product-compliance
Ingram Content Group UK Ltd.
Pitfield, Milton Keynes, MK11 3LW, UK
UKHW041831100926
8556IPUK00002B/121

9 781839 990823